The Lucayan Taíno
First People of the Bahamas

Also by Sandra Riley

Homeward Bound: A History of the Bahamas to 1850

Bahamas Trilogy: Miss Ruby, Matt Lowe, Mariah Brown
A Collection of Historical Solo Dramas

Sisters of the Sea:
Anne Bonny and Mary Read—Pirates of the Caribbean

Sometimes Towards Eden: Anne Bonny in Jamaica

Stone Poems/Wotai: Help on the Way

The Greenbear Chronicles

With Peggy C. Hall

Gus Greenbear and the Beijing Fortune Cookie Caper

The Lucayan Taíno
First People of the Bahamas

Story
by
SANDRA RILEY

Paintings
by
ALTON LOWE

PARROT HOUSE
2017

PARROT HOUSE

The Lucayan Taíno: First People of the Bahamas
Copyright © 1991, 2005, 2013 By Sandra Riley (text) and Alton Lowe (paintings)

ALL RIGHTS RESERVED. No part of this publication may be reproduced or transmitted in any form or by any means, electronic or mechanical, including photocopy, recording, or any information storage and retrieval system now known or to be invented, without permission in writing from the publisher, except by a reviewer who wishes to quote brief passages in connection with a review written for inclusion in a magazine, newspaper, or broadcast.

Library of Congress Cataloging-in-Publication Data is available upon request.
ISBN#978-0-9846191-2-2
Parrot House Softcover Edition Published April 2017
Printed in United States
First published as *The Lucayans* by Macmillan Education Ltd. London and Basingstoke, 1991
Parrot House Hardcover Limited Edition published December, 2012

Cover: *Night Sun* an original oil painting by Alton Lowe

Book designed by Frank Wendeln

The film *Full Circle: A Taíno Story* © 2012 The Crystal Parrot Players

Visit our website
www.crystalparrot.org

Acknowledgments

For the Macmillan Edition 1991
Alton Lowe and I extend our thanks to the following people for their advice, assistance and support: Liz Basile, Mary Jane Berman, Dan Blackmon, Robert S. Carr, Mike Donovan, Don and Kathy Gerace, Gotthard Bank, Julian Granberry, Peggy C. Hall, Davidson Hepburn, Terry and Barbara Herlihy, Charles Hoffman, Sr. Dorothy Jehle, Tony Leicester, Joe and Millie Lleida, Eugene Lyon, Dianne Machado, Barbara Magnanini, Vanessa Magnanini, Sue Nelson, Anubis Perez, Cecilia Rennella, Miriam Rosen, Margie Salem, John Saunders, Jim and Virginia Schrenker, Oscar Seiglie, Joe Shi and John Winter.

Permissions to adapt and include research material gathered, thanks to:
- Richard E. Buhler of the Brotherhood of Life, Albuquerque, New Mexico for allowing me to share Col. Churchward's *The Sacred Symbols of Mu*, (1988).
- Farrar, Strauss and Giroux, Inc. for "The Beginning Life of the Hummingbird" from *The Red Swan: Myths and Tales of the American Indians*, (1976).
- Little, Brown & Co. for Columbus' Journal entries from their book *Admiral of the Ocean Sea* by S.E. Morrison, (1942).
- The Otto G. Richter Library of the University of Miami Special Collections for the Bachiller 1883 and Zayas 1914 dictionaries.

For the Parrot House Revised Edition 2012
I wish to thank Peggy C. Hall for her infinite patience proofreading the text over and over again. *Gracias* Luisa Black for translating the report of "The Expedition by Canoe from the Amazon to the Caribbean Sea," submitted to the Academy of Sciences of Cuba by Antonio Nuñez Jiménez. To Alex Zacarias for his film *The Lost Taíno Tribe* and for his efforts to document United Nations symposiums and Smithsonian Museum workshops, radio interviews and ceremonies, *bómatum*. This invaluable compilation of research material pertaining to archaeological, historical and contemporary Taíno culture can be accessed on his website: www.thelosttainotribe.com. Thanks Michael & Maryellen Lopez for showing up at every event. A big thank you to Alton Lowe for his support over the years and generosity in providing new works of art. Thanks to Chris Dale for photographing Alton's paintings for inclusion in the book and to Frank Wendeln for bringing back the brilliance of the colors in the original paintings. Thank you James Mastin for creating the Taíno sculpture. Endless thanks to filmmaker Travis Neff for his work funneling all the research and creative efforts presented in the book and the play into a synergy that became *Full Circle: A Taíno Story*.

List of Paintings and Acknowledgments

Page	Painting	Owner
5	Nature's Pilots - Detail	Gotthard Bank
6	Lucayan Taíno Vessel	Gotthard Bank
9	White Sand Beach	Artist's Collection
10	Rocky Shore	Iris Lowe Powers
12	Lucayan Taíno Village	Gotthard Bank
14	*Strombus gigas* (Queen Conch)	Private Collection
16	The Potters	Gotthard Bank
19	*Argusia gnaphalodes* (Bay Lavender)	Private Collection
22	Emergence	Sir Orville Turnquest
25	Spirit of the Waters	Gotthard Bank
30	*Encyclia gracilis*	Private Collection
31	*Bletia purpurea*	Private Collection
32	The Fishers	Gotthard Bank
34	The Fishers - Detail	Gotthard Bank
35	*Tellina radiata* (Sunrise Tellin)	Private Collection
36	Bahamian Parrot - Detail	Dr. Ulrich Baench
37	High Cay Guanahaní - Detail	Mel Schenweather
39	Bahamian Parrot - Detail	Dr. Ulrich Baench
40	Bahamian Parrot	Dr. Ulrich Baench
42	Cliffs	Artist's Collection
51	Night Sun - Detail	Gotthard Bank
56	*Bidens pilosa* (Shepherd's Needle)	Private Collection
57	*Chicocca alba* (Snowberry)	Private Collection
58	*Encyclia cochleata*	Private Collection
61	Lucayan Taíno Traders - Detail	Gotthard Bank
62	Sunset	Artist's Collection
64	Lucayan Taíno Village - Detail	Gotthard Bank

PAGE	PAINTING	OWNER
65	Night Sun - Detail	Gotthard Bank
67	Night Sun - Detail	Gotthard Bank
68	Night Sun	Gotthard Bank
71	*Coccolba uvifera* (Seagrape)	Private Collection
72 (top)	*Guaiacum sanctum* (Lignum Vitae)	Artist's Collection
72 (bottom)	*Encyclia plicata*	Private Collection
73	Misty Sky - Detail	Private Collection
74	Misty Sky	Private Collection
82	The Bluff	Artist's Collection
85	Discovery - Detail	Gotthard Bank
86	Hatuey Ascending - Detail	Artist's Collection
88	Men from Heaven	Gotthard Bank
90	Discovery	Gotthard Bank
92	Nature's Pilots	Gotthard Bank
94	Island Rocks	Artist's Collection
97	*Chrysobalanus icaco* (Cocoplum)	Artist's Collection
98	*Byrsonima lucida* (Guanaberry)	Private Collection
100	*Eugenia rhombea* (Red Stopper)	Artist's Collection
101	*Manilkara bahamensis* (Wild Dilly)	Artist's Collection
102	*Tabebuia bahamensis* (Five Fingers)	Private Collection
104	Lucayan Traders	Gotthard Bank
107	Thanksgiving	Gotthard Bank
123	Hatuey Ascending	Artist's Collection
132	Columbus Monument San Salvador	Gotthard Bank
163	Junkanoo Romeo & Juliet	Artist's Collection

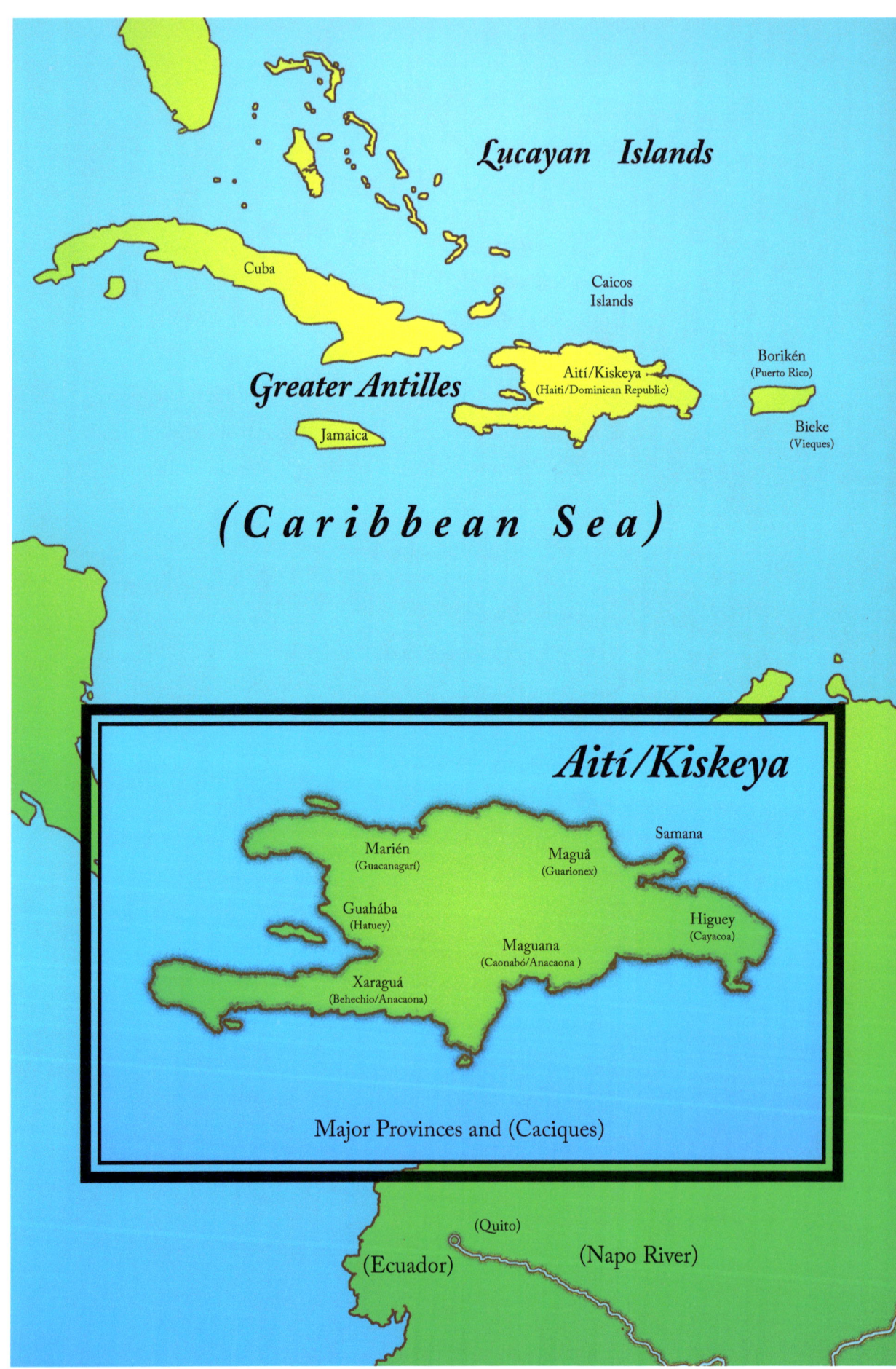

Lucayan Islands
Bahama
(Grand Bahama)
Lucayoneque
(Great Abaco)
Bimini
Nema
(New Providence)
Sibateo
(Eleuthera)
Habacoa
(Andros)
Guanima
(Cat Island)
Guanahaní
(San Salvador)
Korateo
(Exuma)
Yuma
(Long Island)
Samana
Mayaguana
Haomate
(Crooked Is.)
Inagua
Lesser Antilles
(Margarita)
Cubagua
(Trinidad)
(Venezuela)
(Orinoco River)
(South America)
(Negro River)
(Guiana)
(Brazil)
Path of the 1988
Scientific Expedition
by Canoe
(Amazon River)

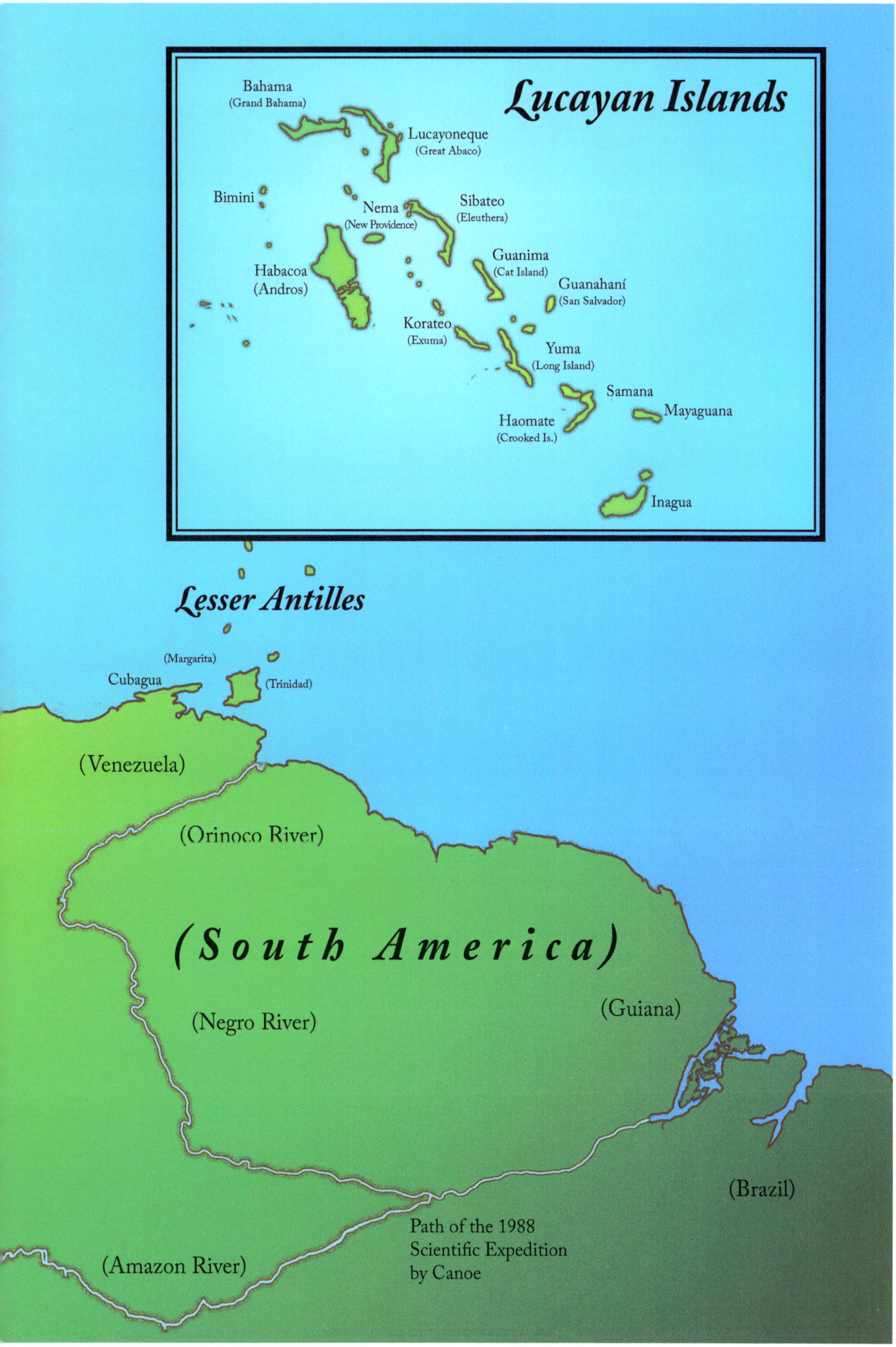

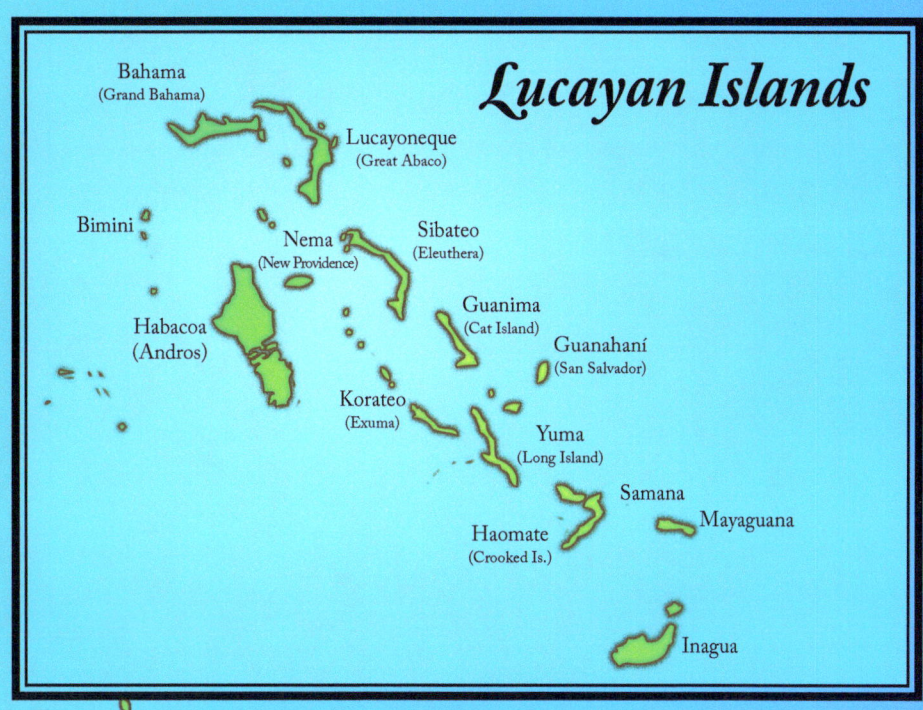

Author's Preface

Before and since the 500-year celebration of Columbus' arrival in the Bahamas, there has been a resurgence of Caribbean archaeological and linguistic research. Among the many publications, Julian Granberry's *Languages of the Pre-Columbian Antilles* prompted me to revise the novella and glossary of this book. It also aided in creating dialogue for the film, *Full Circle: A Taíno Story*.

For both story and film one constant remains: the people lived not separate, but as one with their natural and spiritual environments. They saw no boundary between the visible and invisible worlds. The characters in the novella move freely between the world of the mind and body and the world of spirit. Time is simultaneous; past and future are in the present. The narrator of the novella represents the spirit presence of the Taíno people. In the film that presence is a voice. The Man and Woman communicate in thoughts, voiced-over in English. Any spoken dialogue is in Taíno.

As research continues, the Smithsonian Museum of the American Indian plays a major role not only by interpreting artifacts, but also by conducting workshops and holding public symposiums on Taíno archaeology and culture. DNA studies have enabled people to discover their ethnic ties. People are embracing their cultural identity and heritage. Organizations like the United Confederation of Taíno People (UCTP) give them a voice and help keep their traditions alive in the Caribbean, the United States and world wide.

My vision for the novella was to create a greater narrative about the Taíno people through the use of archetypal, universal motifs present in indigenous cultures everywhere that touch our collective unconscious.

Tainotí
Sandra Riley
12 October 2012
Miami, Florida

Contents

   1- - -   The Story
 90- - -   Historical Note
108- - -   Explanation of Symbols
112- - -   Glossary of Taíno Words
124- - -   Bibliography
131- - -   Tracing Steps
       134. .   The *Hatuey*
       138. .   The Play
       142. .   The Film
       151. .   Move Forward…
       152. .   The Sculpture

*Toward having a Taíno Consciousness,
living in peace and harmony
with the earth
and
the peoples of the earth.*

Early Sun

From the sea cliff Father watches.

The Man's eyes are closed. The Woman paints his body.

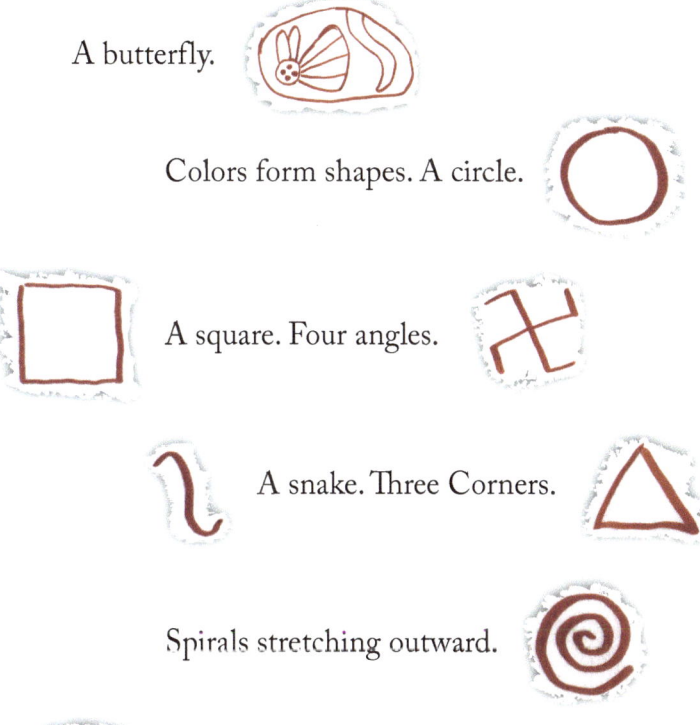

A butterfly.

Colors form shapes. A circle.

A square. Four angles.

A snake. Three Corners.

Spirals stretching outward.

Spirals reaching inward.

Father feels the early sun, smells the earth, hears the builders, tastes the sky. He brings life to the water. Father sees our goings and our comings.

Time.　　All time.　　No time.

The Man drives one foot into the pink-white sand. Time and time again. The Woman's fingers dip red. She traces the longest one down his spine to its root to linger there sliding back and forth like the stroke of a parrot feather. He shivers.

Her palms spread black over his hard thighs inside and outside. On his flattened forehead white lines west to east cut across white lines north to south.

His body quakes like the leaves of the red trunk tree in a storm. His sinews tear. His torso rises and falls like waves in the ocean. His spirit hurls into the sky. He is gone.

Squatting on her heels the Woman waits for his return. He is far away and all is quiet. A rushing wave touches the shore, dry sea grasses scurry along the sand. A red crab scratches near the Man, but he is far away. His screams are lost among the screams of thousands heaved into the fiery air, crushed below tons of stone, drowned in the timeless sea.

```
                              water
                        the
                  above
            lifts
       sun
  The
```

She covers his body with the leaves of the seagrape. A tear drops. She draws a circle on his heart. On the rib below she paints a second circle with a red line from north to south through it. Under his rib she paints another circle and with deep strokes sets two north-south lines.

We begin.

His body jumps as a fish does when it first tastes the bone hook. Tears stiffen in the sea breeze. A smile breaks as she hurls her laughing face into the sun. Prone on his body she listens to the whispers of his breathing. Her breasts feel his heartbeat grow stronger. She weaves her fingers into his and listens.

His pounding heart becomes the thundering reef.

Do I dream? she wonders. No. I am in the sea and very near the reef. Why does he do this to me with no warning? Why do I take his hand?

He sweeps her away from the fire corals and into a feathery bar. Light plays with color. She reaches after the small vibrant fishes. The sun falls into the water and pours over her face. She darts in spurts of elation. They float. Her hand locks in his.

Under the water her hand looks large. Her laughing face sustains him, but he often thinks of her hands. Soothing hands, yet strong. Strong enough to hold him when he feels himself split. She gathers the pieces of him like corn. A hummingbird has hands like these, he thinks. Small. Quick. Strong.

She touches a filmy creature. It is breathing with its whole body as she does when she is underwater with him. Drift away from him and her throat becomes the burning of a thousand cooking fires. She thinks, I want to feel that. I try to pull my hand out of his grip to see what he does now. A great cliff bird holds me, I cannot break away. I frighten him.

I know he frightens me when he goes away without me. When he goes and leaves his body with me. My spirit flies when he takes my hand. I want to go to the great island to the west under the oceans in the sky where we gather herbs and flowers. So many colors, so many plants—all watery green. The sun does not burn them like here. Why, I wonder? And the light is like the setting sun all the day. Why? I will ask Father. He knows.

        A

            sudden

                drop

Atop a white cliff the man they call Father, with arms outstretched, lifts into the air. As a great bird he hovers over the circle of deep blue in the green-white sea.

The ring of light at the water's surface is high above them now. Like a whorl they spiral down

        sinking

            falling

Let go of fear, his touch tells her. This is not death. Shake off death. He looks up. Only a speck of light, smaller than a grain of sand, remains. She seems calmer now. Her hand on his forehead tells him—no more words.

His life-giving force enters her life-nurturing place. In the deepest darkest watery tomb they create life.

She ascends, dragging his lifeless form. There is life inside her. She cannot follow him. The pull from above is strong, the weight of him cannot carry her down.

He wills to die. Dark and cold. Let go and fall into the everlasting.

Light widens and spreads its mantle over them. Pink-white like the seed of the conch.

Her hand breaks the surface and is clutched by the claw of the great bird. They soar and dive and spin then descend floating to the shore.

The Man falls into Father's arms.

"Bring us water."

Leaving the Man and Father on the white beach, she runs into the sun and wind to the village.

A cup of water. It is a simple request. Bring water to bring back life. A twig breaks under her foot, lizards scramble in the bush. What vessel to use? A gourd? A clay cup? What size? What shape? What pattern? What colors?

Be quiet and listen. A voice shouts in her head.

The morning sun enters Father's hut placed where two rows of houses cross. Shadows dance on the reedy wall. On a limestone shelf the vessel sits. A shore bird perched atop two small gourds. Its beak pecks the earth.

He is this vessel. I am this vessel. I can give life back to him.

At the pond beyond the village, she pushes the vessel into the standing sweet water and feels herself fill up.

14 February 1492 Castile

The mass is beginning.

Júdica me, Deus, et	Judge me, O God, and
discérne causam meum	distinguish my cause
de gente non sancta.	from the nation that is not holy.

I am on my knees as I have been since Your Majesties received the seed of my plan to reach the Indies by sailing west. I pray my enterprise will grow nourished by your favor as you prosper in the favor of Rodrigo Borgia, Alexander VI, our Pope.

The priest is lifting the chalice and making the sign of the cross with it. Unworthy though I am, I must prepare to receive the Body and Blood of Our Lord and Savior Jesus Christ.

Sanguis Domini nostri	The Blood of our Lord
Jesu Christi custodiat	Jesus Christ preserve
animam meam in vitam	my soul unto life
æternam. Amen.	everlasting. Amen.

Cristóbal Colón

Father receives the vessel and with both hands raises it to the sky. He flicks a few drops of water onto the sand, then dips the tail of the bird into the Man's mouth. Laying a hand on the Man's heart he waits.

She takes up the vessel, plies the gourds to warm the earth's blood. Blowing across the opening, her rich, deep note summons his spirit.

Body warms. Breath quickens. Blood drips through the fingers of his right hand onto the sand. A gash spreads across his palm from wrist to forefinger.

She drops the vessel.

The Man opens his eyes. His smile drains as he looks at his bleeding hand. Eyes quicken, scanning his memory for a lost dream.

"Woman, take up his hand."

"My hands fill with blood."

"Scatter the blood in the Four Pathways. Man, heal yourself."

"I cannot. It is too deep."

"A coral cut. Nothing more."

There is something more, he thinks. A long shining object, sharp, thin and bright flashes in his mind.

"Clear your thoughts." Father brushes his palm across the Man's flat brow. Taking the injured hand, he pours what is left of the water over it. They watch the bloody gash close. "Heal yourself. You know how to do that. I am not always with you."

"But you are, Father. Even high on the cay cut by the waves you are with us."

Father places the Man's hand in the Woman's hand. "Deep in the dark-blue waters of the ocean hole the Great Love joins you. Man, you die to self. Woman, you swell with new life. Air and Fire. Water and Earth. When you take hands you fly, you swim, you burn together."

The Man asks. "Does the king approve? Are we of like rank? You teach us many things Father, but you never tell us how we come to be here."

"When you dream, you know these things. It is enough."

"Tell me," the Woman insists. "Who is my mother?"

"I know not. But your father is Hatuey, king of Guahába.

And you are the son of Anacaona, Flower of Gold, ruler of Xaraguá. They govern as *caciques* in Aití/Kiskeya. Go now. Build your nest."

"How, Father?"

"Watch the hummingbirds."

"I see that before, many times."

"I, too, Father. Is it not the same?"

"You are not the same so it is not the same. Nothing stays. Now is all there is."

His voice fades like the song of the morning bird and like a cluster of stars, swallowed in mist, he is gone.

They run along the beach, laughing with the wind, chasing their shadows into the water. The tightness in his chest loosens. The heaviness in her belly lightens. Their arms, like wings, cut the breeze. Jumping over tree roots, they startle shore birds, who sweep their numbers out to sea and swing back behind the couple to protect their nests. They turn back to watch. Near their feet a tern flops and rolls, playing at death. Bursting with laughter, she races down the beach. He springs through the sand after her. Beadmakers look up from their work. Their faces become a blur of smiles. They run long and soft, cushioned by the sand, exhilarated by their bodies' energy, brightened by their own radiant joy. White sand meets gray rock.

They turn inland and drop onto a grassy knoll by a still pond. The silvery leaves of the buttonwood branches embrace them.

The male hummingbird swoops low over the pond. Again and again, climbing ever higher, diving ever lower until the female joins him. Their tails touch—his forked like a split branch, hers rounded like a river rock.

Soft whirring. Streaks of green and white and violet flicker from flower to flower, dart at specks.

Hovering over her hand in lightning stillness, a bird's tongue extends to taste her fingertips. Finding no nectar in her dye-red fingers, it beats away.

All about them now, sparks of green irradiate the woody pond.

"If we beat at their speed we can fly to the stars."

Reaching to touch his lips, "First learn to build our nest here." The birds bring bits of cotton to the branch, both male and female knit their nest.

    Woven tightly.
        Thickly feathered.
            Rounded perfectly.

The birds bring leaves to cushion the hard sticky floor.

"I make mats of palm for our floor too," she whispers. "And weave a tight *hamaca* which you hang from strong posts."

The energy of the busy wood charges the air. A yellow butterfly lights on a water flower in the pond and flutters slowly.

Mornings.

Hutía is cut up and made ready for the daily stews. Women split the meat with knives of *manatí* bone. In every village around the island, in every season, women slice *hutía* with *manatí* bone for the pepper pot and thank the small creatures for their sacrifice. All the mornings.

Morning songs.

Gather salt from the shallow ponds. Gather spices for cooking, herbs for healing, cotton for nets. Gather fruit. *Guayaba. Papaya. Banana.* Dig up the *yuca,* roots of the *yucubia.* Sing. Scrape. Grate. Squeeze out the poison. Sing. Bake our bread. Sing. Make our wine. Gather the wood from sick and dead standing trees. Wood to make our fires dance. Posts to make our houses strong. Boards to cut for oars. Logs for *canoas* to carry us over the ocean to trade. Wood for the bow and arrow shaft, throwing sticks and harpoon to fly and strike on our hunts. Wood to make music. The music of reeds stirring in the wind, a soft, high bird song, wind whirling through ocean caverns, the whoosh of bats leaving the cave at dusk, the beat of the rumbling waves, light scented breezes ruffling the trees. Hunt with us. Dance with us. Sing with us.

Father takes up a conch, breaks off the top, puts the hollow tip to his lips and blows two notes in summons. On the bluff he stands. The ocean pounds the rocks below.

The Man and Woman come to him. They kneel and touch one hand to the ground, then to their foreheads in greeting. "We are ready for you to light the new fire."

Wood brought by people from every part of the island is carefully laid. Once lit, villagers come and take these embers to light their home fires. Fire tenders keep these embers hot for many days, many nights.

"Woman, go and ask that tree which straight branch it honors itself to give for our whirling stick. Man, find a strong flat board fit to receive the shaft she makes."

Father kneels beneath a thatch palm, broken conch shells spread before him. The Man returns. Then the Woman. They kneel to face him. Father curls his fingers inside a fragment of shell and smooths his thumb over its battered ends. With both hands he raises it to the sun. "You feed our bodies with your flesh. Your shell touches every part of our lives. The Great Worker sees what you do all day, every day. Your cups hold our water. Your spoons hold our food. Your swallowing sticks purify us. You weigh down nets, dig sand, chisel wood, gouge limestone, chip coral. You drill and scrape and notch and grind. You are our cooks, our potters, our fishers, our farmers, our artists, our priests."

Father takes a pinch of crushed shell used to temper clay to make vessels and griddles. He puts a flake on his tongue. The Man and Woman do the same. "*Taínotí.* We are one."

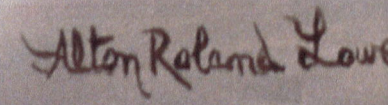

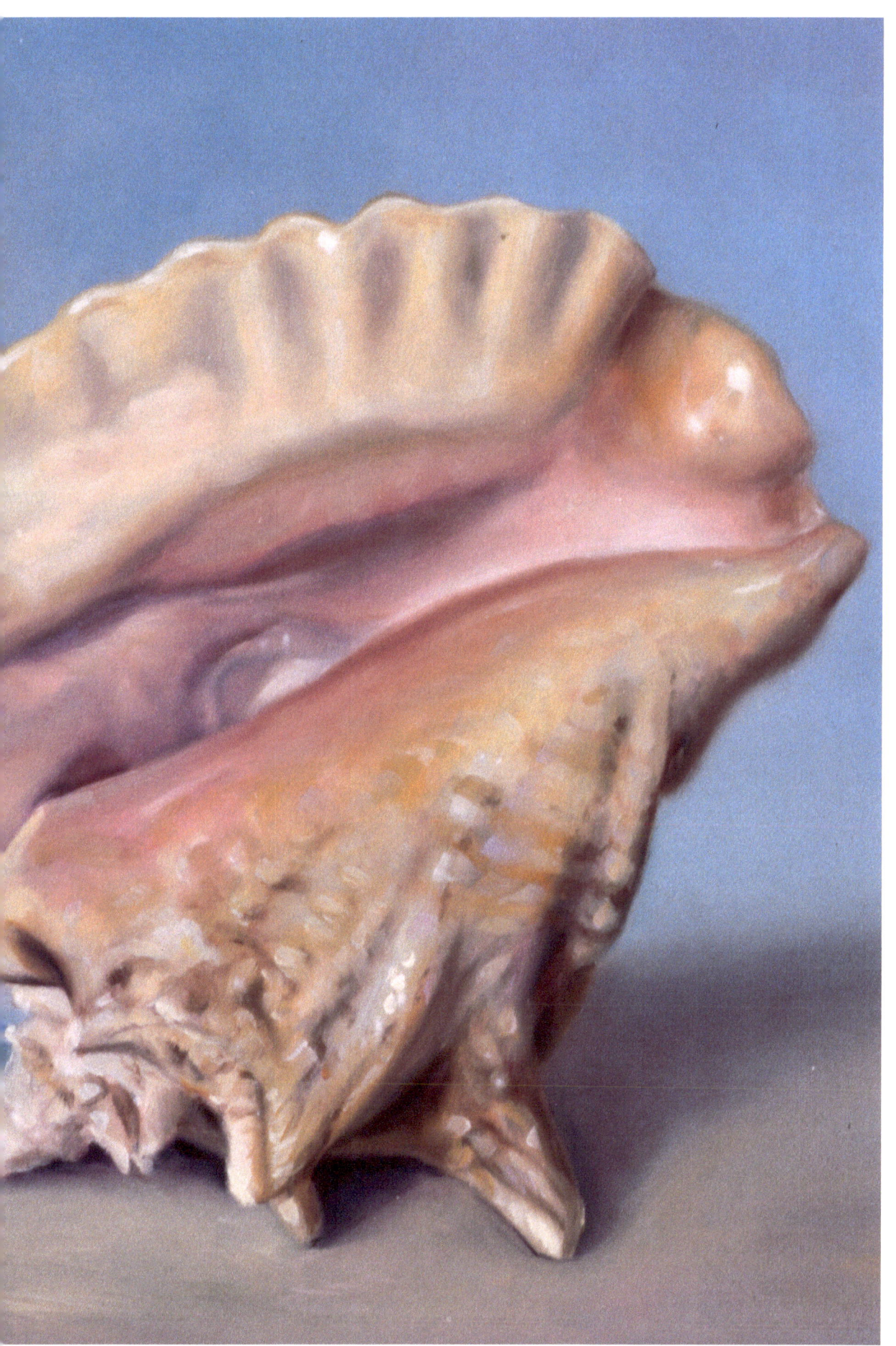

The Woman takes up a jagged tool and scrapes with even strokes up and down the long fire stick. The Man takes a gouge and first tests the hardness of the board. Pushing gently, he loosens the wood and readies a circle to receive the action of the whirling stick.

While they work the wood, Father chooses a pointed shard. On a thick round shell fragment he scratches the likeness of the Mother of the Moving Waters. Eyes wide. Breastless. Fists thrust under her chin, elbows pressed to her sides, legs drawn up. Birthing.

    Scrape
          Gouge
                Scratch
   Smooth
        Rub
            Polish

The Man kneels and sets his foot on one end of the flat board. The Woman puts the fire stick in the prepared place. Spinning the stick between her palms, she works her hands firmly down the shaft. When she reaches the bottom, the Man begins his motion, pressing and moving his hands back and forth down the spinning stick. When he reaches the base, her hands are at the top again. Whirring in a steady rhythm, they kindle.

Tipping the embers into shavings of dry bark and cotton, they softly blow the tinder into flames and lift their arms to the sun.

"Does it anger the Great Fire in the Sky when we take a piece of it?" she asks. "The people think so and shake with cold in the night rather than make a fire."

"The life within you takes its food from you. Does that anger you?"

"No, I ..."

"What is your deepest fear?"

"I do not know, Father."

"Find it."

She looks at the Man whose eyes follow a snail carrying its tiny conical house over the pitted rock.

"He cannot help you. He holds his own fear." Father listens and watches the changes in her face. "This is the morning. Your body is sleek. Its glow shines into every eye. Do you fear that in the afternoon when you grow big like the earth that no one can see past your outside self to the inside Self that sparks that light?"

The Man looks up. The golden flecks in her brown eyes warm him and he falls within their rings.

"You take his hand."

"But I do not know why."

"Sensing is knowing. Knowing is sensing. Can you feel him inside you now? He is there. Swimming with your child. You are soft this morning like the water flower. Other mornings, most mornings, you are the fleshy plant that shoots its darts at everyone who comes too close. See this Man's body, pierced all over with your yellow spines. Do you wish me to take you to the interior where you can be alone to cry for yourself?"

"How can I be alone? He is inside me and a new life is inside me."

Father snaps his fingers. "He is back now. You can rid yourself of this child. Any of our women can tell you how. Then you can be alone."

"I am ugly like the prickling plant."

"He tastes and finds you radiant. Your child tastes and finds you healthful. Taste of your own red fruit." He fingers a cord of cotton dotted by small, round, flat pieces of shell. From it hangs the lumpish figure of the All Mother. "I have made something for you. If you find her ugly squatting there, do not take her up."

Father takes from his neck the cone-shaped image of the All Father, The Provider, Giver of Yuca, Giver of Life.

The Man extends both hands to receive the *cemí* made from one of the humps encircling a conch shell.

Father ties to the middle of his own forehead the figure of The Dog, wide-eyed, whose male part reaches his chest, whose fists press under his chin, whose elbows grasp his sides. "We draw our strength from these. This is for you, young master, to give bread to the bodies and spirits of our people. For me, a guide for my spirit once I leave this body in death. And you, the courage to give birth alone." The Man feels the heat of his loins penetrate the cold dark water and he is alone. Father flies with the Spirit of Darkness and he is alone. Hearing the spirit song of the All Mother in the trees, she feels the pull of life and she is alone. The chunk of shell sweats in her small fist. She ties it around her neck. "Like the arms of the love vine, our lives entwine. *Taínotí.*"

19 March 1492 Castile

The priest sings the first words of the mass. We chant the antiphon.

Introíbo ad altáre Dei.　　　　　　I go unto the altar of God.

Waiting. Waiting. Waiting. My Queen, I fear you have deserted me. On my knees before the statue of Our Most Blessed Virgin I pray your gracious Majesties will give your royal permission for my expedition. I require only three or four caravels equipped for exploration and ask only a portion of revenues from the trade in the Indies for myself. Since this is the holy season of Lent, I shall fast and pray until I hear from you. I shall fast until Easter, even to the Feast of Christ's Ascension if I must.

The mass is ending. The priest is chanting the last gospel of St. John.

In princípio erat Verbum, et Verbum erat apud Deum, et Deus erat Verbum. Hoc erat in princípio apud Deum. Omnia per ipsum facta sunt: et sine ipso factum est nihil, quod factum est: in ipso vita erat, et vita erat lux hóminum: et lux in ténebris lucet, et ténebrae eam non comprehendérunt.

In the beginning was the Word, and the Word was with God, and the Word was God. The same was in the beginning with God. All things were made by Him, and without Him was made nothing that was made: in Him was life, and the life was the light of men, and the light shineth in the darkness, and the darkness did not comprehend it.

　　　　　　　　　　　　　　　　　　　　　　Cristóbal Colón

People gather on the pink-white beach facing east to sing the morning songs, to dance the morning dances, to chant the morning chants, to kiss the air.

A flurry of plumed bodies soar, swoop. Sideways and backwards sweeps of green, white, reddish-brown and violet. Children with baby feathers dance with hungry mouths.

They chant.

> h'm MM h'm MM h'm MM h'm MM

The First Bird hovers. Sips the flowers in the headdress of the First Father. Sips the flowers growing from His sacred fingers.

> h'm MM h'm MM h'm MM h'm MM

Out of the Darkness He grew. His Thoughts His Sun. He lights the world by His Own Inner Self.

All lips meet the air and separate.

> pha PHA pha PHA pha PHA pha PHA

He is the First Wind.

> pha PHA pha PHA pha PHA pha PHA

Butterfly sing.
Sing to the scattered vapors. Bring them whirling into order. Carry this, the First Command of the Creator.

> Drum beat. Pipe sound.
> Heart pound. Earth pulse.
> Shake the shaker. Live the story.

Sing the song of the Dreamer Who Makes. The crawfish makes the earth. Dance the dance of clawing sand, of scooping mud. From the ocean's floor build an island. Make a world.

> Earth breathe. Sing. Dance.
> Dream the First Dream.
> Sing in the Sun, the Moon.

Dance the first dance of the sun and moon. Out of the first cave the sun and moon fly into the sky.

Sing the song of the first people who live in a paradise inside the hollow earth. No sickness. No pain. No death. No sun. One man comes out into the darkness and returning too late is carried off by the sun. Hide from the sun. Close the cave. Outside the man is turned to stone. By the door of the cave sits a stone. One stone. More people come out to go fishing. They are taken by the sun and turned to trees. Another man goes out to find the soap plant to wash himself. The sun catches him and changes him into the bird who sings the sorrowful

morning song. Dance the dance of the rocks and trees. Sing the songs of the birds and creatures of the earth.

    Chant the chant.
    Go with the sun. Return with the sun.
    Nothing ever dies.
    Go with the sun. Return with the sun.

Drum beat. Heart beat.
ta TA ta TA ta TA ta TA
Pipes sound. Shells clink.
sha SHAKE sha SHAKE sha SHAKE

Sing the song of the separation of men and women. The man does not return with the soap plant. He is the morning bird. An angry man says, "I will leave this cave and search for other lands. Women, leave your husbands and take gemstones." He carries off the women to Matinino and leaves them there alone. The island of women. Alone.

The men left behind bathing in the water want women. They search for women in the rain. Eel-like creatures fall from the trees. Swift and slippery they speed away. The men catch only four and wonder what creatures these might be with no parts of male or female. Eels with arms and legs. They tie up their arms and legs and bind a woodpecker to them. The bird thinks they are logs and bores a hole. The wheel of life begins.

Chant the chant.
The Creator is One. Becomes two.
Makes three and four and five.
We begin.

Sing the song of the sea. A cacique buries the bones of his son within a great gourd and fastens it to a beam in his house. One day he comes and takes it down. Opening it, whales and other monsters of the deep come forth. He tells his people not to come near this gourd for the sea is contained in it. Four brothers, whose mother died at their birth, come to the gourd to get fishes. The great man returns. In their haste to hang up the gourd it drops and breaks. The sea rushes forth over the plains and valleys leaving the mountain tops. Our islands.

Dance the dance of the sea.
Dance all the morning long.
Chant the chant.

Sing the song of the great cacique, *our first chief who sees our sickness and pain and looks for a way to calm the Unseen Spirit and ease our suffering. Our first leader walks by the sea. The Spirit of the Waters rises from the waves. Talks to him. Teaches him. She gives him a gourd, a holy calabash with four white pebbles. Shake the gourd. Dance the dance of the Unseen Spirit. All the mornings, he chants the chant. And after a life of wisdom and goodness he does not die. He goes up.*

Chant the chant. Dance the dance.

Do not die. Go up. Go up. Up.

Do not die. Go up. Up. Go up.

Do not die.

GO UP

Full Sun

The arrows of the sun meet the arrows of the earth.

The Man falls to his knees. He is alone. After the dancing, after the singing, after the stories, the others go off to the midday meal. He is fasting. Half-buried, a chunk of dead coral glints white in the sand. Across the flat rocks in the sea he finds another piece of coral, one rough enough to use as a grater. As he begins to work the coral, he can see the bird inside. He can feel the curves of its rounded body heavy in his hands. Its beak rakes, ruffling its feathers. Its tail points to the sky.

She comes to the beach to fling fish bones into the sea. Back to the beginning. Our beginning. Out of death comes life.

Winds from the east carry sounds harsh and unfamiliar.

The man is too absorbed in his carving and does not hear what she hears.

Voices chanting in a language she does not understand. Why is this distant music drifting here?

The unborn one hears this singing. Do not fear, you are safe inside me.

Shake away fear.

In the crystal ocean he sees the blues, greens, and reds of the parrotfish as they dart after the bits of fish falling from her fingers.

He takes the coral bird to her.

She lifts the bird into the sun.

He kneels, rests his face against her rounded belly and listens. He listens to the beat of life. Warm and safe with the world in his arms, he watches bubbles on the water's surface reflect as stars on the sand beneath. Dancing stars. A perfect world. Does the unborn one feel the sun, smell the air, hear the bird, taste the fish, dance with the stars? He wonders. Yes. Woman as mother is the world—all the lands and seas, sun and moon and stars. Life is all there is.

"Are these stars I see in this coral bird?" she asks.

"Yes."

She draws his face to hers. His eyes are as dark as the red-brown wood. She thinks, When I have hurt him in some way, he does not look at me. He walks by with his eyes to the ground. I feel empty then. When he is angry his eyes turn black. In his anger he shouts at me, "You have golden stars in your eyes." The words sting like the bite of the sand fly, yet I laugh. This makes him angrier and he screams, "Your hair is shining." She laughs until he smiles. She kisses his smile.

18 April 1492 Castile

In preparation for Holy Mass my voice startled the priest as I sang out the *Vidi Aquam* for truly this day I "saw water flowing." Our agreement, yet to be confirmed, was signed. I thank Your Catholic Majesties for the promise of caravels, titles, and tithes. Don Cristóbal Colón thanks you. As Admiral of the Ocean Sea I thank you for my ships. As Viceroy and Governor of all the lands I discover, I thank you for the tenth of all the gold, silver, pearls, gems and spices found or acquired by trade in said lands. Above all I am grateful for your blessing on my voyage. The hard work begins. I pray God give me the strength to attend to the outfitting of my ships and the courage to win souls for heaven.

Cristóbal Colón

    The day grows full. Father, standing on the highest hill, watches, loves his people, blesses their tending. All around the island, they farm in black land and red land and white land. Grow *tabaco* and arrowroot. Plant the shoots of the *yucubia* in the red land. Draw up a hill around the slanted plants. Heap the earth around the shoots. Sift the grated *yuca* to make the bread of life.

    In the white land plant *maíz*. Push in the fire-hard stick to make a hole and drop in the seeds. Sing the song of the field. Tie our hair with strips of *iguana* skin. Strips cut with *iguana* face bone. Plant *maíz* in the new moon. From an *iguana*-skin sack take seed kernels, the gift of the Great Spirit, brought from Paradise, the Motherland.

    To bring rain, carry two ropes across the round pond in the center of the island. Father looks down. Where the ropes cross, toss in gems and gold and sweet smelling herbs. The Woman drops a blue stone into the pond.

    To harvest, gather crops into baskets of silver thatch. Cover them with sweet-smelling flowers and all the flowers that feed on the air. Sing the first fruits. Celebrate the harvest. All the harvests.

Fishers make nets and basket traps. Watch the spider weave its web and make a net. Take boats out to the reef, set lines and traps for grouper and snapper, grunt and shark. Send the fish to find and ride the sea turtle, draw it in. On the shore dig for clams. Catch the crab. In the shallows strike with spears.

At the mouth of the bird lagoon, the Man stands in the flats.

Spear in hand he stands so still his shadow disappears. He waits. A streak of red. He strikes deep.

He scrapes the scales off his fish with a shell decorated with the sun's rays.

She is a fisher too. She can hit a parrotfish with an arrow. He hears the squeal of parrots and knows that in the bush young boys are snaring them. He remembers. *Hiwaka!* I catch the first one who answers my call. Its cry brings more birds. It is easy then for a few boys to loop many parrots. We sit in the tree and one by one the birds drop to the ground. The earth beneath us is all green and spattered blue and bright red.

The bird struggles in my hands. My heart hammers my chest. Let me go. *Hiwaka* speaks to me to set it free. Free in flight or free in death. I am its terror. I cannot soothe it or let it go. In times past I lie in the bend of the tree of life and parrots come to me and talk to me and let me stroke their red throats. That is why I am chosen to catch the first parrot. No more. All the parrots on all these islands know me now. Know how I lie. Bird, you are sacred. Bird, I need your feathers to make a mantle. Bird, you will dance. Dance. Dance. Dance. I twist its neck and scream. All the islands hear my screams. The bird is silent. I lie back along the branch and rest the parrot on my heaving chest until I am calm. We die to live again. I take all your feathers for my mantle and we dance. I open you and use you for the paste to hold your feathers to the cloth of my mantle and we dance. I take your bones to a high cliff and hurl them into the sky and you fly again.

He looks up from scaling his fish. Several canoes enter the water. Many men and boys paddle to the high cay and to the low cay to hunt the *iguana* with dog and stick. He wants to join them, but she is waiting in his canoe.

The sun is full. She ties a band of cool cotton across his forehead.

"Trading boats approach the north end of the island. We must greet them. Father wishes it."

He sees the water vessel resting on a strut. The bird sitting on two gourds. Its water revived him one morning as he lay on the white-white sand in the early sun. She tells him that Father says, "This sacred vessel comes from a great land to the north. It must go back. Now is the time. And this." She places in his hand a figure of white stone not much bigger than his thumb. "This *cemí* must go to the north where the spirits go."

He lets his finger trace the features of the tiny figure's double ringed eyes, large flat earlobes, belly, absent a button, and the feet turned backwards.

As they paddle out of the inlet, he can see the people on the high cay. The hunters look like small brown wood doves moving in a line across the island. Force out the *iguana* and batter it with your sticks. Dance away from its tail that can slice a man's belly. Skin it. Cut up the meat. Put it in a pepper pot. Season with *ají*. Mash up the rest of it. The *iguana* is tasteful and gives strength. The *iguana* skin keeps babies warm in the seasons of cold. The *iguana* has three eyes.

They round a point of sand and paddle up the western coast of their island, Guanahaní. The third eye of the *iguana*, what does it see? What does it know?

Gliding through a narrow cut near a green cay, they push across the harbor to the shore where many large canoes are pulled up. On a point of land, cut in two by the action of the sea, Father looks down on them.

Traders come to Guanahaní from great lands and islands north and south and west. From near and far they bring the green stone axe, salt and *tabaco,* plants for skin dye, spices and herbs, the rubber ball for our games. For each our people give many parrots and darts and balls of cotton, all they have. Once for three pierced seeds of the conch the Woman traded many things.

Canoas of all sizes carry gourds of all shapes, leaves and black beans of the plant used in the *cohoba* ceremony. *Cemís, coco,* pearl beads from Cubagua, a thin, black stone sharper than any bone knife and a fish hook made of gold.

A trader from Lucayoneque has a gemstone, bright green like the sea. The Woman hands him the bird vessel. For some beans used in the *cohoba,* the Man gives him the white spirit *cemí.* There are no words. The man gets in his canoe and paddles to The People's Distant Waters Land. Alone.

Hurry. The sea is changing. A big force is coming. Hurry away from Guanahaní, our island. Take a calabash of water and a portion of the bread of life. Ride swiftly over the waves to Lucayoneque, your island.

22 July 1492 Palos

It has been eight weeks since I arrived in Palos and we are almost ready for the adventure to begin. Our crew numbers ninety men. The two caravels, the *Pinta* and the *Niña* and the merchant ship *Santa María* have been fitted out for exploration. We have readied all our charts. Rations are now being laid in: wine, a good biscuit, oil, vinegar, salt beef and fish, cheese, lentils, chickpeas, honey, rice, almonds, raisins…

Cristóbal Colón

On the point of land cut by the sea, they lie in the swirls of smooth limestone. The ocean rages against its bounds and rushes into the caverns beneath. They feel the earth shake and hear the music the sea makes piping in the hollow chambers. The wind riffs in the trees. Light dances through the facets of the bright green stone. They listen to the music of the island.

The sky is changing. The sea is changing. We are changing. Everything changes. Nothing stays.

They pull their canoe high on the beach, climb to a ridge and look back over the bay and rocky point where the music stays.

Down the path to the inland lake her small canoe waits in the tall grasses at the water's edge. He gathers gourds and lines for hunting ducks and she takes her bow and quiver of arrows for shooting birds.

Tossing in many calabashes, the Man enters the water. Through the circles cut in his gourd mask, she can see his eyes move. She laughs and wonders what the ducks think he is and if they think that he, along with the other round gourds, are their own kind. Swimming among them, he snatches a foot and ties a duck to the rope around his waist. Two, three, four, five in all.

The Woman hunts one bird from the many long-legged, snake-necked creatures sifting their dinner from the mud of the black mangroves. One *biáya* smoothing the black tips of its coral wing feathers stands apart from the flock. Here are feathers fit for a *cacique's* headdress. She decides to shoot the bird rather than chase it down. Her arrow is true. Its point kills, but does not tear. No blood to stain the light-red feathers. The other birds, startled, move away. She steps carefully, silently, lifts the bird into her arms and retreats.

They do not see me, she says to herself. I walk near them and still they cannot see me. Sometimes when the shadows pattern the west bank, but do not fall on me, I can touch them. I can stroke their feathers. Feathers the color of the flush of dawn. As a child I would run among them, just to see them fly. How wonderful to see them fly. Now I wait all day to see them fly.

One day as a child a dark force fills me up. It moves me to hurl many darts among these birds. They rush one way then another before crashing into the mangrove. Father turns my darts into the water. No bird is hurt. Their cries and shouts break the peace of this quiet place. After, Father does not look at me. For days and days he does not look at me. My crime is great. I feel a hurt inside every time I see these birds. The hurt of many darts.

She places her bird in the canoe next to his catch.

Suddenly all is still. No birds sing. No palms stir. No crabs scratch over dry leaves. It is too quiet. The stillness holds them.

Light flashes in the dark sky. Paddling smoothly, they wind their way through the arms of the lake, down its narrow chest and stomach into its bowels. The growing wind sends fluffs of brine skittering along beside their canoe.

There is something more. They sense fear. The fear of many? The fear of one? They are not certain. Somewhere on the island, someone is afraid. Where? Near this lake? A boat caught by the waves off to the east? They pull their canoe to shore and run along

the path, cross the inlet in another boat and reach the village at the head of the lagoon. They hurry to the bluff and stare into the new fire. Four logs in the limestone depression meet in the center and point in the Four Directions.

"We cannot look in all Pathways. Look into the center with me," he asks of her. "If we can find our center, the calm inside us, we will know which way to go. Point to the log that shows the direction we must go."

She points to the south.

"Yes. But I see no *canoa* out there." Shifting his eyes to the west. "There. The trouble is on the cliffs. We need help."

"But everyone is gone into the caves. They fear a big force. We must go alone and take with us long, tough lines."

The inlet waters are smooth. The wind fattens and pushes into the white bay where the water heaves. Their flat bottomed canoe glides over the low places and rides the waves neatly.

"Crying. A child is crying. Our child hears it."

On a high cliff a boy finds a sea hawk's nest.

As he explores the roots of plants turned to stone, a piece of the ledge breaks off and crashes into the sea. The child falls. They look down and find him clinging to a rocky shelf. Ocean waves rush over coral heads and lash the white stone.

Tying the fibrous cords under her arms she steps down the crusty limestone. The child is small and light. From above, the Man lifts them up and lands them safely in the fleshy leaves of the bay cedar that grows along the ground atop the cliff.

The rain beats and the wind cuts.

Waves blow up through the caverns to swamp them. The boy wants to join his people at the Beadmakers' Village. They have memory of a blur of smiling faces as they run in the early sun.

The storm swells. Branches fall across the path, the many paths crossing the island. At the pond of the hummingbirds, they watch the petals of a water flower pull up and take flight in the wind. There are no butterflies.

They climb into a cave to wait. The driving rain, the lashing wind, the loud sky are quieted in this place.

The Woman scratches on the side of the cave with a twisted piece of broken conch. Gouges the lines of a face. Outlines a broad forehead and narrows the face down to a pointed chin. She scratches cross hatch lines between the slanted eyes and over the nose. Atop his head a crown.

"A great *cacique?*" asks the boy.

"My father Hatuey, ruler of a Taíno kingdom in Aití. I see him in dreams and even if the earth should move and break up this cave, he is here."

3 August 1492 Palos

We embark this day. Our casks are filled with sweet water from the fountain near the church. Every man and boy is with me now in the church of St. George. Since no priests will sail with us, it is our last opportunity to confess our sins, receive absolution and the Holy Eucharist.

We repeat the words of the priest.

Confiteor Deo omnipoténti ...   I confess to almighty God ...

I think back over the many years I dreamed and planned for this moment. I intend to keep a journal of every particular of the voyage of discovery to present to Your Majesties on my return. I remember the day the Moorish King kissed Your Royal Hands and soon the Gran Can of the Orient, the King of Kings, will renounce his idolatries and heresies and accept the Holy Christian Faith.

… quia peccávi nimis cogitatióne, verbo et ópere …	… that I have sinned exceedingly in thought, word and action …

Yesterday the Jews were exiled from this city and all your realms and dominions.

mea culpa, mea culpa, mea máxima culpa.	through my fault, through my fault, through my most grievous fault.

Soon I will weigh anchor, leave the harbor of Palos for the river of Saltes...

Indulgéntiam, absolutiónem et remissiónem peccatórum nostrórum tríbuat nobis omnípotens et miséricors Dóminus.	May the almighty and merciful God grant us pardon, absolution and remission of our sins.

...sail South by West to the Canary Islands, then due West across the Ocean Sea to the land of the Gran Can, King of Kings.

Amen.	Amen

Cristóbal Colón

On the white-white beach of the western shore the people gather to sing the songs of the full sun. They form circles along the stretch of sand. Circles of elders. Circles of men.

Circles of women. Circles of children. All repeat the phrases of the Man, a leader, their *tekina*.

Song of the Long Long Past

Before the sun. Before death.
Before the ocean falls from the sky.
Before we come from the Land of the Sun
The Motherland of man.

Ships like arrows sail on lights.
We talk in thoughts.
Music is language.
The rhythm of breezes and tides.
We move through doors in the earth.

Country of wide plains and soft hills.
A feather mantle of green covers the land.
Over all the land four rivers flow.

In tall trees birds with bright feathers sing.
Butterfly. Hummingbird.
Spicy herbs. Heaps of flowers.
Big-bellied gourds. Tall corn.

Seven cities. Great houses of stone.
People—white and yellow and brown and black.
Sail all the oceans of the world.
From the eastern ocean to the western ocean.
From the northern to the southern seas.

Monsters with small heads on long necks roam
Tearing up the green of the earth.
Clamping in strong jaws plants and bush and trees.
Flying monsters too, swooping up other monsters.

In the night the earth rolls and shakes.
Fires heave and spurt.
The sky breaks.

Some float to nearby shores.
To the east of their flooded land they go.
Others go farther east to the Great South Land
Across the Great Lake to the Great Land
In the western ocean.

The circles of elders, of women, of men and of children now repeat the phrases of the Woman, a leader, their *tekina*.

Song of the Long Past

The builders have memory.
They build again.
They build another paradise.

Some people eat each other.
Many starve and die.
Too many white-haired people
Grunting and shaking their spears at us.
Run from them. Fly from them.

Go away from us white-haired people.
Go north away from us.
Far to the north and east.
East of the Great Land in the western ocean.

The Great Land in the western ocean splits.
It sinks and drains our Great Lake into a river.
Mountains rise up in our plains.
Leave the city of gold by the lake.
Find another paradise.

Father as a sea hawk swoops low and scatters the circles of dancers and singers. "Never again sing of the city of gold by the lake." Father stands on the beach. He takes the Man's hand in his right and the Woman's hand in his left. The people form a straight line and repeat Father's phrases.

Move forward by stepping backward.
Dance the dance. Trace our steps.
Sing with me.

Song of the Tracing Steps

> Follow the Great River. Tracing steps.
> Life after life. Tracing steps.
> At the Black River wind northward.
> Live along the Gentle Flowing River.
> Life is easy. Life is kind.
>
> Move east out of the mouth
> Of the Gentle Flowing River.
> Move west. Live from island to island.
> West. Home again? No.
> Go north now. To Guanahaní.
>
> Move forward by stepping backward.
> Step backward. Move forward.
> Forward. Backward.
> Move forward by stepping
> Backward.

Why backward? In a trance, the Man drifts out of the line. Where do we go when we move forward by stepping backward? I must know. What is the next step in the dance? Where does the song end?

Father is gone to the point of land at the north to fast and pray for forty suns. I go into a cave. I want to see the time beyond this time. Father knows where I go. He sees what I see. The Woman wants to see the island as the birds see it. She is the fish hawk there in the sky. Father flies where she flies, sees what she sees. When she swoops over him, he does not look up.

The Man listens to her thoughts and hears her say, "Why think about time past or time ahead? There is no time but now. Why bury yourself in a cave with our ancestors? Come with me. Look at the reefs protecting our island. High in the sky I can see Father on the point of land cut by the sea and to the point of sand to the south. See the great water in the middle of our island. See how much faster I reach the cliff where we found the child in trouble. I see him now standing with his fish net in the shallows of the inlet. Red fish like stars in the water all around him. He waves to me and speaks to me. As a child I spoke to the birds. Our child talks to birds. I climb higher and can see all the islands. There is our ocean hole. I swoop down over it."

27 August Las Palmas, Grand Canary

We have been in these islands many days now. The *Santa María* is a slow sailer. I must repair the *Pinta's* rudder and re-rig the *Niña*.

I am very busy here and have no time to inquire about the situation on these islands. I have heard talk that two conquistadors have been falsely accused and sent home in chains. Some say the Spaniards, through treachery and cruelty, enslaved the Canary Islanders and forced them to convert to the Catholic Faith. I am sure these are but rumors.

Cristóbal Colón

From the beach he watches her fly. She climbs into a cloud shaped like the spreading wings of a great bird. It is the image of her as she is now. She is safe inside herself.

He runs. The sun burns deep into his back. The sand scorches his feet.

Father speaks. "To look beyond, look within."

"I am afraid. The cave is dark."

He crawls inside to where he can stand but stays on his knees, trembling. Bats veer from him. In the middle of the cave is a small clay-like hill. The Man sits on top of it. He sets his water bowl in front of him. A bowl of her making, with handles shaped like frogs. He flicks a few drops in the Four Directions and sips the water.

Full suns. Deep in the cave, the Man does not know how many full suns he waits atop the rocky mound. His stomach twists, his throat aches. Burning pains strike every muscle. His head pounds.

The mind holds many worlds.

Breathe out one world.

Breathe in another.

 His body quakes like the leaves of the red trunk tree in a storm. His sinews tear. His torso rises and falls like waves in the ocean. His spirit hurls into the sky. He is gone.
 He opens his eyes to fearful sights and sounds. Everywhere there is motion. Strange noisy objects with people inside dart by him. Overhead, monstrous birds with shiny gold tail feathers tipped blue and black roar and streak across the sky. Buildings grow tall like trees. Where are the trees? Along the too wide paths the bush is black, their leaves are black, their flowers are black. Smells mix to turn his stomach.
 A terror wells up in him. White-haired people in bright clothing come toward him. Their garments are dyed and patterned with the stamps women use to decorate their bodies—birds and flowers and turtles. Lines and figures that we put on our pottery. These white-haired people are young like me. Why am I afraid? They dance and laugh like I do when I drink too much of the wine made from *maíz,* and stumble like me when I sniff the *cohoba*. The world turns upside down for them too. What is their reason for drinking? Where is their ritual? They beat each other, rape their women and break their sacred vessels. There is no cleansing in their vomit. What visions do they see when they fall down and sleep in the sand? What do they learn in their trance? Where have they been? Where are they going? They are like the white-haired people of the long past, jumping up and down, grunting and growling and throwing spears at us. Have I come north? I must leave this place.
 The Man is lifted up, pitched and dropped into a muddy field. The earth around him is ripped and scarred. Trees and bushes are broken and pushed aside like some giant beast had clawed, scooped and pulled the vegetation out of the earth then flung it aside. He digs out a small white stone, half buried in the dry earth. It is the spirit *cemí* he gave the Lucayoneque trader. He drops it on the ground as he is swept up and carried to another place and dumped into another ruined forest.
 He sees tracks, strange tracks unlike any animal he knows. Are they the tracks of the monster who spoiled this land? He follows. High on the hill he sees the water. The same colors of the sea surrounding his island. Can this be? He climbs a tree. This island is much smaller than his island and he can see other islands close by—trees dwarfed and land barren. Have the beasts come to all the islands?
 Down the hill the path widens. It is wider than any path needs to be wide. Trees and bushes and wholesome plants are piled high on either side. Shiny objects stuck in the withering branches are the fruit of these dead trees. Rumbling noises shake the earth. Loud, rattling sounds. He stalks closer and sees the beasts. Golden like the sun.

Growling, choking and grinding, the long-necked monsters bend and snatch up all the green bush. In every direction they turn and bite the earth. Other short-necked monsters with wide mouths push the trees aside.

Some creatures eat red clay. They chew the earth and spit mouthfuls into hills.

Clamping, tearing, crushing, vomiting earth and rock. On circling banded feet they crawl. One is close by him now. On its hide is a drawing. Two lines within a circle.

This picture tells me this is only the beginning. These monsters make more monsters to rape the earth on all the islands. I cannot breathe. There is no air here. The smoke from these beasts chokes me. I am killed.

On the tail of one beast is a picture of a sleek creature with branching horns leaping into the air. I do not know this animal but I can jump the way it jumps. There is hope in the jump. He leaps into the air and when he wakes he is kneeling on the mound of dripping rock. The vessel is overturned.

He fumbles for the vessel and raises it to his cracked lips. The last drops of sweet water taste bitter. Slumping onto the rocky mound, he lies prone, arms outstretched, eyes shut against the splinter of light falling on his face.

Senses battered.
        Body knotted.
                Heart empty.

Night Sun

Leap to a star.

Leap like the hooved, horned creature into the sky. The stars are our only hope.

11 September 1492 The Ocean Sea

I watch the stars. I tell the time by Polaris and navigate by the North Star. Cipangu is on the same latitude as the Canaries. Of the eight winds Japan lies West. The ocean between the Canary Islands and Japan is short, only 750 leagues. If we miss that island we will surely reach mainland China, our primary destination.

This is the third day since we last saw land. The weather at sea is like Andalusia in April, but here there is no song of the nightingale.

Every evening I pray to Our Lord and Savior Jesus Christ to spare us from storms and calms.

Cristóbal Colón

The Woman talks to the plants, asks questions of the bushes and the flowers. They respond by telling her their many uses, their many pleasures. She comes to the white bay near the high cay with her basket of soap leaves and fragrant plants to wash.

    The Man uses a swallowing stick and coughs up what appears to be the black juice of the poisonwood tree. He staggers into the water. The stick floats out to the open ocean. His body is covered with the grime of that other world. His nose is filled with its smoke and soot. Lathering the leaves of the *digo* plant, she rubs his tight shoulders. He feels like the yellow-green matted vine which grows in aimless directions in and out, up and down and around itself.

    She is filled with her adventure. Filled with the wonder of their island, shaped like an egg with a body of water inside—lakes and ponds and blue holes. Clothed in forest and mangroves, hills and cays. Guanahaní is like the earth, the Great Mother. The lakes and ponds are her blood and she turns herself, first one side then the other, to the sun to warm herself.

"From the sky I see a great *canoa* coming." Her fingers work the lather into his hair. Her excitement dims in his silence.

The sun drops.

He tries but cannot find the words to tell his vision. There is no language for it. No music, no song, no dance can tell it. The gulls and terns screaming and fighting over bits of bread is a piece of that world. Parrots squawking to the aid of one of their own is part of it. He tries to tell her about the monsters who eat up the land but she cannot picture them.

"I must fight the yellow beasts. They are ten tens my size, still I must find a way to destroy them."

"Where is the wisdom in that?" She crushes the petals of a fragrant flower and smoothes them over his face and neck.

"If we cannot change the time beyond this time, we will choose another."

21 September 1492 The Ocean Sea

We have been in the Sargasso Sea several days now. The ocean is a rust-green meadow. Although the men are fearful of being stuck in the weed, I keep a straight course.

Cristóbal Colón

    Canoes round the sandy point and glide up the western coast. Many flat boats come from other Lucayan Islands. From Bimini, the island of the healthful spring, to Inagua, the island of the pink birds. From Lucayoneque, Bahama, Habacoa, Guanima, Yuma, Samana, Mayaguana, Caicos. She could name them all, ten tens of islands in every direction. Yet, no canoe ever comes to Guanahaní from the east.

    Hatuey steps from his *canoa* and approaches Father. The Man is on Father's right and the Woman on his left. They kneel and touch the sand, then their foreheads. The sun falling behind the great *cacique* glints on his headdress, neckpiece, belt and armbands.

    "So you are the Man who holds the heart of my daughter.

You are radiant like your mother, Anacaona, Flower of Gold. I sense her wisdom and feel her tenderness in you. I hear her poetry, her songs. Her spirit dances with your spirit."

    Holding his daughter close he says, "Blessings on the unborn one."

    The Woman smiles and looks at the red-orange circle in the sky. All look. The ocean which rages against its bounds and swallows the rain is waiting now to quench the Great Fire.

    All along the beach the people stand. A line of people stretch northward and southward. Along the sandy beaches and the rocky shore they watch the sun.

She is frightened. The falling sun always frightens her. She takes hands with the Man and Hatuey. They move into the line of people on the long stretch of beach.

Father, knowing that the body is thought, goes with his thought to the village of his birth on the northwest point to stare at the sun. With a splendor all around him, Father chooses to go with the dying sun.

All the people, the old and the very young, sit on their heels, rest their elbows on their knees and face the palms of their hands toward the ocean. They stare straight into the sun and with gaping mouths they call. Summoning croaks, rasps, and screeches from the back of their throats they shout their farewell. The bellowing, hooting, squawking continues until

>   flashing green
>   the sun
>   drops
>   into the sea.

It is the moon of the first fruits. In a village near the head of the inlet on the eastern shore, Hatuey rests on a *duho* carved in the likeness of part man, part lizard. On his head he wears a headdress of seven pointed fragments taken from the conch.

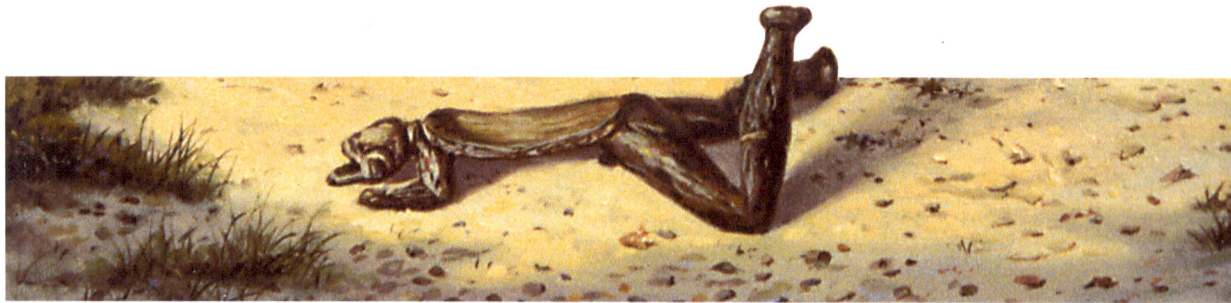

On the ridge along the beach all the houses glow in the yellow moon.

Inside, *hamacas* with sleeping children swing beside hanging baskets with the bones of their ancestors.

From all parts of the island women come to present the first fruits of the *yuca* harvest.

Seated on his honored place, Hatuey watches women lay their gifts all around him. His daughter is among them. Big with child she kneels behind her basket of *casabe* made from roots planted, nurtured, gathered, squeezed, grated, pounded and baked by her own hands.

The women dance the dance of the first fruits. They dance with the outside of their hands turned outward. The *cacique* watches as the subtle movement of their feet sets their hips to swaying and listens to the tinkling shells on their ankles. But it is the hands that speak to him—smooth, graceful, the backs always facing him, fingers stretching, looping towards him. These hands tell of his generosity, his authority, his vitality. They tell of the many gentle, loving kindnesses he bestows.

Receive, great cacique, *these our gifts
The first fruits of our fields, of our wombs
All the fruits.*

When the dance is ended the women take their baskets of bread to a large open place where the people wait. In a *hamaca* chair, men carry Hatuey to the plaza. He blesses the bread, breaks it and gives it to the people.

In a loud voice he speaks. "Take to your houses this bread, the gift of the Great Spirit. Keep it for twelve moons to protect you from the big force with the lightning that shatters trees, the wind that tears our roofs and the rains that drown our crops. From these and other dangers protect us."

The people chant the name of the Great Breath, the Creator, The Giver of Life.

*Huracán Hu racán Hura cán Huracán
Hura cán Hur a cán Huracán Hur
a cán Hura cán Hu racán Hura
cán Hur acán Hur a cán Huracán*

The Man has memory of his vision and wonders, *All* other dangers?

6 October 1492 The Ocean Sea

Martin Alonso Pinzon thinks I have passed Japan. He urges me to change course to SW by W. I fear I may miss mainland China, the land of the Gran Can, King of Kings.

The men are restless. Almost two weeks ago we mistook the sky for land. I know we have passed the island the Portuguese call Antillia—the seven cities. But I must not miss China where the roofs are made of gold.

Cristóbal Colón

Night

In the night, plant crops by the moon, parts of moons, the twelve moons. At the new moon women plant *maíz*. Fast and feast. To cleanse our bodies, use the swallowing stick of wood, of shell, rib of *manatí*. Drink the black drink. Sniff and sneeze. Purify our bodies to receive the spirits, see the visions, know the signs. At ceremonies and festivals feast and drink. At times when the moon and sun disappear, feast and drink. At times when the sun rises casting its longest light, feast and drink. At harvest festivals feast and drink.

At night, the light of other worlds bursts forth overhead. A wide roadway of stars stretches across the sky, the path of the soul at death. At night. All the nights.

10 October 1492 The Ocean Sea

    Three days ago I changed course WSW. Forty petrels flew by our vessels in that direction. A boy hit one bird with a stone.
    At night we hear birds and see them in flocks so large they shadow the moon.

Cristóbal Colón

    The Woman looks up at the full yellow moon and has memory of other nights. On the night before the night we take hands the Man leaves me standing at the north point. He turns his back and walks away into the darkness. I stand and wait for him to circle the island and return to me. It is necessary, Father says, for him to leave me so that we both can feel the sorrow and the joy of life and love, for all the days in one day.
    Father knows the signs. He tells us it is time to tie ourselves, each to the other. That although the Great Love blesses us, it is necessary to perform the ritual with the people present.

"In the moon when the seagrape leaves turn red you must take hands. You, woman, see the man in you, and you, man, see the woman in you. This is knowledge."

She has memory of only pieces of that night. At a rocky point of land at the north end of their island she and the other women carry baskets of pots covered with flowers—the yellow of the rock flower, the pink of the dogwood, the tree of life and all the flowers that live on the air. The yellow moon hangs low over the bay. Before the men come, the women break the pots.

By the light of the night sun they break all the pots in all the baskets. Sing the song of breaking pots. Dance the dance.

The moon disappears and the men come. Beat the drums, pipe the pipes, shake the shakers, rattle the gourds. The fire burns bright. Dance the fire round. Keep the fire on our right. Dance round and round. I stand on a high place with the Man and Father. Hand in hand we stand, our necks encircled with ropes of scented white flowers. The fire blazes beneath us. The air chills, a thin mist covers the stars, the moon disappears. The people lift their eyes to heaven in amazement. Lit from the fire below, the shadows of our forms appear above us. Hand in hand we hang in the misty sky.

11 October 1492 The Ocean Sea

Yesterday the crew was mutinous. I told them that we would turn back if we did not find land in two or three days. I promised the men I would not abandon them to an unkind fate and at vespers invoked the Blessed Virgin Mary to protect us.

Since sunrise we have had many signs of land. The *Niña* picked up a green branch loaded with little flowers like our dog roses and the *Pinta* found a small wooden stick which looked as if it had been carved with iron.

Cristóbal Colón

"Where is Father?" She asks the Man as she prepares his powder for the ceremony of the *cohoba*. "Did you look for him?"

"He is gone to another world. His body is buried in the forest surrounding the dance circle." He has memory of his vision. "It is best."

"For him. What about us? What about the one soon to be born? The child needs him."

"You are angry with Father. Are you afraid to give birth alone?"

"I have fear."

"Maybe Father chooses death so that the unborn one might live."

"Hatuey gives me the stone for painless childbirth at the ceremony of the first fruits and goes away. Father gives me the symbol of Atabey, the All Mother, and he leaves me."

"It is our way for women to give birth alone. I cannot be with you in body, but I am with you."

"It is a hard thing."

In the turtle-shaped bowl she crushes the beans and leaves with a parrot-shaped pestle. She places the powder in the small gourd he wears around his neck and ties the feather mantle, decorated with pearl beads, around his shoulders. He turns in a circle before her.

"I am ready to receive the visions of the *cohoba*. That too is a hard thing."

11 October 1492   The Ocean Sea

At sunset I changed the course from WSW back to W. I do not know why. I gathered the men together for evening prayers. We said the *Pater Noster*, *Ave María* and the *Credo*. I led the men in the Litany of the Saints. After each intonation they chanted in Latin the response, "pray for us."

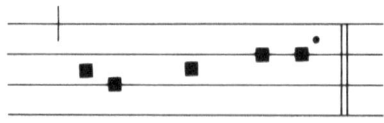

Sancta María - ora pro nobis
Sancte Joánnes Baptísta - ora pro nobis
Sancte Joseph - ora pro nobis
Omnes sancti Angeli et Archángeli - orate pro nobis
Sancte Michaël - ora pro nobis
Sancte Gábriel - ora pro nobis
Sancte Raphaël - ora pro nobis

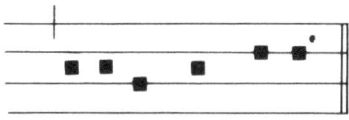

Omnes sancti Patriárchæ et Prophétæ - oráte pro nobis
Sancte Matthæe - ora pro nobis
Sancte Marce - ora pro nobis
Sancte Luca - ora pro nobis
Sancte Joánnes - ora pro nobis

Omnes sancti Mártyres - oráte pro nobis
Sancte Damiáne - ora pro nobis
Sancte Laurénti - ora pro nobis
Sancte Vincénti - ora pro nobis
Sancte Stéphani - ora pro nobis
Sancte Sabastiáne - ora pro nobis

Omnes santæ Vírgines – oráte pro nobis
Sancta María Magdeléna - ora pro nobis
Sancta Cæcília - ora pro nobis
Sancta Catharína - ora pro nobis

Omnes sancti Innocéntes - oráte pro nobis

Cristóbal Colón

At the dance plaza the people gather. Four poles are placed, one at each of the Four Pathways. Dressed in leaves and feathers and carrying branches and flowers they dance. The men, arms on the shoulders of the men on either side, move in one direction. Women, their arms resting on the shoulders of the women on either side, move in the opposite direction. Behind them and all around them in the forest beyond them, the spirits dance.

Dance of the Spirits

>Drum beat. Pipes sing.
>Shells clank. Gourds rattle.
>From left to right. From right to left.
>Dance the dance of the spirits.

The Man steps forward, clothed in the feather mantle set with pearls. The singers and dancers repeat his chanted phrases and his steady movements.

>Trace the steps of the Taíno
>People of courage. People of peace.
>From the heart of the Great South Land
>Along the Gentle Flowing River
>Out and around into the Sea
>From the Little Island to Borikén
>To Aití, home of the Taíno—Bohío,
>Land of the fresh flowing rivers.
>
>Aití. Land of great chiefs.
>Guacanagarí, *cacique* of Maríen
>Guarionex, *cacique* of Maguá
>Cayacoa, *cacique* of Higuey
>Caonabó, *cacique* of Maguana
>Anacaona, *cacique* of Xaraguá
>Hatuey, *cacique* of Guahába.
>
>Life is gentle. Life is good.
>Trade with other islands.
>Jamaica, land of woods and streams.
>Cuba, land of the wide valley.

Dance the dance of tracing steps.
Saomete takes us north.
Takes *yucubia* shoots and herbs,
Healthful plants to grow again.
Inagua, Mayaguana, Samana, Guanahaní.
Gentle islands. Our new home.

11 October 1492 The Ocean Sea

We sing the *Salve Regina,* each of us chanting after our own fashion, for mariners are fond of music.

Hail, Holy Queen, Mother of Mercy, hail, our life, our sweetness and our hope! To you do we cry, poor banished children of Eve! To you do we send up our sighs, in this vale of tears! Turn, then most gracious advocate, your eyes of mercy towards us; and after this, our exile, show unto us the blessed fruit of your womb, Jesus! O clement, O loving, O sweet Virgin Mary!

Cristóbal Colón

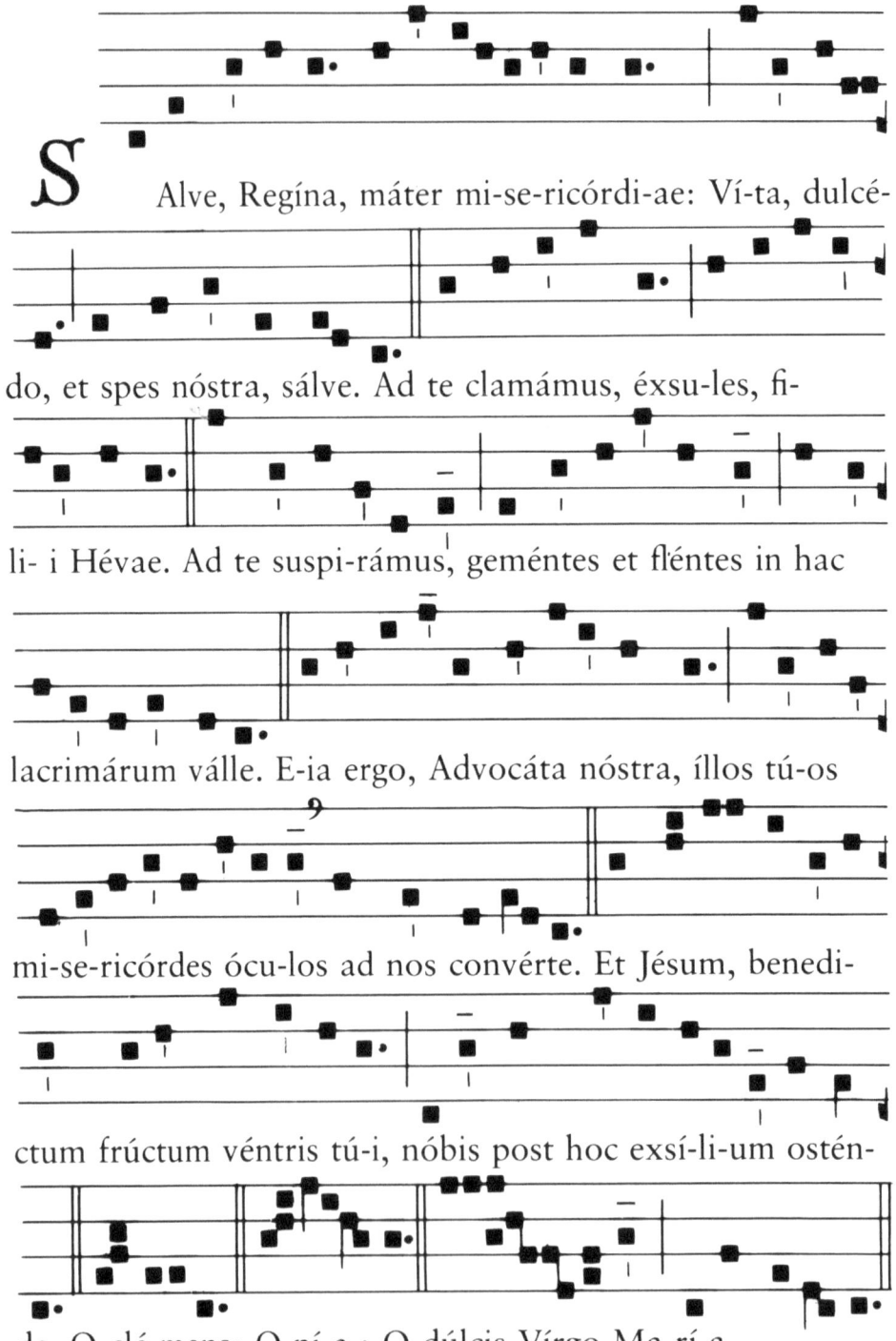

Night Songs

> Night songs sing of the day.
> Beat the drum. Drink the wine.
> Dance to the rhythm of our singing.

The Child from the Beadmakers' Village moves behind the circle of men and the circle of women to offer wine from an owl-shaped vessel.

> Chicha Chicha Chicha Chicha
> Step in time. Step in time.
> Step together. Step. Step.
> Chicha Chicha Chicha Chicha

The Woman steps forward, big with child. The rhythm of her movements swings slow then fast. The others follow in perfect time. She sings.

> *The child leaps to life. Father leaps to death. Feel what I feel. Dance with me. This night I come upon a bird fallen from its nest. I hear an owl nearby. Waiting. In my hand the bird makes a little sound and opens its mouth wide to me. It cannot live. One eye is bloody, its beak is broken. Leave it to the owl. Nature's way is best. But will death come quickly from the owl? Will the baby bird be frightened? In my hand it is not afraid. It need not know of fear. I cannot let it suffer. I snap off the head with bloody eye and gaping mouth and bury it. The owl denied the pleasure of the kill, denied this bite of food, flies screeching off. If death must come I can do the killing.*

The dance builds to a frenzy. The Woman big with child leaves the circle and goes into the wood alone. The men leave the women to their wild dancing. They go to the bluff to the *cohoba*. The Man touches his naked chest and knows the weakness of the fledgling. He thinks about the Woman big with life going off alone to give birth to their child. He hungers to know what that feels like. Do other men ponder these things?

The feathers of his mantle tremble in the night breeze as he walks the path to the bluff. The moon is the moon that ends the season of storms.

The Man is thinking about storms. Storms between people. Storms inside the self. She holds the stone of painless childbirth and the spirits are within her circle. Still I wish to be near her, to help her struggle. Just as there is a struggle in death, there must be a struggle in birth.

At the *cohoba*, fires blaze and flare when the men place palmetto leaves on it.

11 October 1492 10 PM The Ocean Sea

Only the boys are asleep. All the men are watching. I take a sighting of Polaris. When I look back to the horizon, I see a light which looks like a wax candle rising and falling.

Cristóbal Colón

The men, faces painted red with *bija,* sit around the blazing fire. Taking a stick from the embers, the Man lights the tightly rolled *tabaco* leaves, puffs and blows the blue smoke into the stars. "To *Huracán,* the Breath of Life, the Great Wind, the Heart of the Sky." Then he sends smoke along the Four Pathways.

He pours the dust, crushed from the beans of the *cohoba,* into the turtle-shaped bowl and using a forked reed sniffs the powder three times. The feather mantle weighs like stone upon his shoulders. He is warm inside. He can feel his blood running through his veins. The earth spins and the stars appear at his feet.

In his vision, a tall man stands before him, silver spun in his golden hair. He wears a long white robe strewn with red crosses like flowers. Pointing toward the east, his blue-white eyes hold a warning. The Man is drawn into those eyes.

Spinning through space, he is hurled forward in time and dropped into a river overflowing its banks with his own people. Unable to run, he stands terrified with them as brown-robed men pour water on their heads and make the sign of the Four Winds over them. Suddenly strange men wearing bright breast covers ride into the river atop wondrous four-legged creatures. Lifted up, the Man hovers over the scene to witness the horror as these men with their shiny-sharp sticks slice and hack at the people. Heads, limbs and bodies drop into the bloody river.

Plucked away, he falls into another place where dogs hunt his people and tear them to pieces. *Caciques* are hanged by the neck with their feet barely off the ground, dangling in fire. Nearby, the strangers stab babies and feed the wriggling bodies to their dogs.

In another place, he sees a man tied in a great fire built with spears. Flames lick his body. A man, robed in the color of the earth, stands holding a pole, its top crossed with another stick. The burning man turns away from the cross, lifting his face to the sky.

"Hatuey!"

In a *cacique* village he sees a radiant woman carried in a *hamaca* chair. Flowers fall from her arms as she is brought to meet these strangers. Baskets of gold she sets before them. In another place and time he sees this same woman dragged to a dance plaza and hanged before her people. They shout in terror. "Anacaona! Anacaona! Anacaona!"

"Mother!"

In a remote place the Man sees his people in despair jump from cliffs, drink the poison juice of the *yuca,* throw themselves onto sharpened sticks, club their children to death, and hang themselves from trees. Everywhere his people hang in trees.

He sees the Woman standing over their sleeping child. Her arrow points at its back. Death is quick. She buries the child under a bitter *yuca,* safe from dogs. When he looks up he sees his wife hanging in a tree.

"No!"

How can this happen? Why does this happen? When is this happening? Flying among the stars, twisting and turning through levels of time and space he cries out for her. He sees her standing alone in the tall trees which line the beach on the west coast of Guanahaní. The white beach where she breathed life into him with the sweet water. How beautiful she is waiting there, golden in the early sun staring out to sea.

He looks where she looks. Just beyond the reef are large *canoas* riding high in the water. "Boats from the east," some say as they run to their canoes, to paddle out to greet them. "Men from heaven," other young men say as they go to trade with the white-skinned men on the beach.

Is this where it starts? Here at Guanahaní? He walks toward a tall man who is standing near a large cross his men are planting. His eyes are drawn to the tall stranger's shiny stick. The man smiles and reaches the stick to him. He grabs the blade and cuts his hand.

Writhing on the ground in front of the fire he screams out all his warning, all his pain. The pain of children hacked and mauled, of women raped and split, of men skewered and roasted, of earth clawed and scarred.

Empty of screams and terror, his lungs fill with smoke, the acrid smoke of burning flesh and the choking smoke of burning trees. The Woman unties the string around his throat and the smoldering feather mantle drops into the fire. Flames shoot high into the air, then die quickly.

12 October 1492 2AM Landfall

I look up at the stars to rest my eyes. *"Tierra! Tierra!"* Rodrigo de Triana shouts to me from the forecastle of the *Pinta*. I look and I see what appears to be a white sand cliff on the western horizon shining in the moonlight. Landfall. Thanks be to God.

I ordered sails to be lowered and all vessels to jog off-and-on until daybreak.

Cristóbal Colón

In the white bay under the bluff she washes herself and the child. On the beach he takes her bow and shoots an arrow into each of the Four Pathways. Looking at the mother, he sees specks of light trail from her small hands as she moves them about in the water. Lights of brilliant green-white and blue-white swirl about her and the child. Waves of color and light roll to the shore.

He walks into the star-filled sea and takes the mother and the child into his arms. "We must leave Guanahaní."

"Where do we go?"

"See that star? We will build our nest in that star."

Dance the dance of the unseen spirits.

Early Sun. Full Sun. Night Sun.

Dance the dance. Chant the chant.

And after a life of
wisdom and goodness,
we do not die.

WE GO UP

Early Sun

Historical Note

Columbus discovered America on October 12, 1492. This historical fact has stirred considerable debate over its effects on Western Civilization. It seems pointless to dwell on Columbus' "discovery" when there were people already there to greet him. There may have been as many as one hundred million people in the Western Hemisphere. Clearly, he was not the first man to reach the "New World." Ancient travelers such as Phoenicians, Egyptians, Africans, perhaps even their descendants in other parts of the Eastern Hemisphere, may have preceded him. Columbus did open, or what some scholars might say reopened, trade routes between the Old World and a world new to 15th century Europeans.

Prior to the 500-year anniversary (1992) scholarly debate raged over which Bahama island Columbus made landfall and renamed San Salvador. The Bahamas government decided that for the Quincentennial Celebration of Columbus' First Voyage, the island presently called San Salvador would be the island in the Bahamas Columbus first sighted.

The people who greeted Columbus were the Taíno, the name of the language and culture of the pre-Columbian people of the Lucayan Islands and the Antilles. They called their island Guanahaní.

Columbus kept a journal of his first voyage which details his encounter with the Lucayan Taíno people. After remarking upon their nakedness, Columbus described their handsome bodies, broad foreheads, coarse hair, fine faces, handsome eyes and good stature. They were the color of the Canary Islanders, neither black nor white. The moment he set eyes on the people, Columbus decided that they would make good Christians as well as good servants. This is something Columbus probably thought Their Catholic Majesties King Ferdinand and Queen Isabella wanted to hear.

Bartolomé de Las Casas, a Dominican friar, chronicled the abduction of forty thousand Taíno from the Bahamas to the mines in Hispaniola (Haiti and the Dominican Republic). Kirkpatrick Sale states that the numbers of Taíno who died as a result of European contact by disease, suicide and genocide was not in the thousands, but in the millions. Later, when Conquistadors discovered that the Lucayan Taíno were excellent swimmers, the Spanish took them to Cubagua, an island off Venezuela, to dive for pearls.

According to Las Casas, the Taíno people were by nature good people: patient, humble, peaceable, kind, generous and affectionate. The word Taíno means good or noble. During the forty years he lived at Hispaniola, he watched them die and described the hideous manner of their murders in his book *The Devastation of the Indies*. Oviedo wrote of "cruel deaths as uncountable as the stars."

The Lucayan Taíno thought the Spaniards were taking them east to an island where they would be reunited with their ancestors. In actuality, the Spaniards took them to Hispaniola and slavery. Unlike the Spaniards, the Taíno had no proper weapons such as swords or lances, only wooden clubs *(macana)*. However, they did fight when threatened. Peter Martyr writes that when the Spaniards' intentions became clear to them, a few Taíno killed a handful of soldiers with the bows and arrows they used for fishing.

Prior to contact, it may have been tribal warfare that drove some Taíno from the Antilles to the Bahamas before Columbus' arrival. Some scholars believe migration was a result of natural population expansion. In his book, *Languages of the Pre-Columbian Antilles* (2004), Granberry traces migration patterns as part of his study of the archaic language sources and the development of the Taíno language in the Caribbean. Archaeological evidence gives support. Prior to the arrival of Columbus, Classic Taíno was the lingua franca of the Bahamas and Greater Antilles, with the exception of the northwestern peninsula of Cuba.

Little is known about the lifeways of the pre-Columbian people. Early Spanish historians, who traveled among the various Caribbean Islands, tried to learn what they could before the Conquistadors killed off the people. Oviedo wrote a natural history and Ramón Pané recorded myths and customs. Some information has come from Taíno descendants in Haiti, Dominican Republic, Puerto Rico, eastern Cuba (Oriente), and a few other scattered islands. DNA genealogical research is in progress and perhaps some Bahamians will discover their Taíno heritage.

As archaeological work in the Bahamas escalates and methods improve, the more exciting the information about Taíno lifeways becomes. The Taíno built permanent villages and constructed circular houses of wood and palm thatch. They believed, as did the North American first people, that the power of the world works in circles and that everything in nature tries to be round. Each Taíno family possessed a house which was kept neat and clean. They may have used woven mat partitions, and put flat stones on the ground to keep utensils out of the dirt. They slept in a *hamaca*. Huts faced east to catch the rising sun.

Taíno society was well developed. There was a *cacique* (chief). Following the gold, Columbus attempted to sail to Crooked Island where the *cacique* of perhaps the whole of the Lucayan archipelago resided. Chiefs sat on ceremonial stools called *duhos*, on which zoomorphic and anthropomorphic figures graced the front and geometric designs decorated the backs. Three found in a cave on Long Island resemble one found at Turks Island some years ago.

Caves were used by the Lucayan Taíno for ceremonies and burials. Land was held in common. Like other indigenous cultures, the Taíno believed that land could not be owned, only used. Care had to be taken in its use, for to destroy the land would be to destroy themselves. The Taíno grew sweet potato *(aje)*, corn *(maíz)*, cotton, *tabaco* and the manioc root *(yuca)* for bread they called *cassabe*. Fire-hardened sticks were used to dig irrigation canals and to plant seeds deep in a mound of earth out of reach of birds. Young boys frightened the birds away from the fields. Women did the planting, for they knew how to bring forth life and taught it to the grain.

Lucayan Taíno spent their days hunting, fishing and gathering fruits and berries. Both men and women used the bow and arrow. Archaeologists now think the *hutía* (rodent-like creatures) may have been raised as we raise chickens. They hunted the *iguana* with spears. They fished the *manatí* (manatee), turtle, shark, grouper, parrotfish and conch. They not only ate the conch meat, but also made tools and other utensils from the shell. The parrotfish must have been the particular favorite of one Taíno on Guanahaní. Richard Rose, an archaeologist working through the Bahamian Field Station on San Salvador, found a limestone sculpture of a parrotfish at the Pigeon Creek Site. He conjectured that it was probably a *cemí* (sacred object). It looked like the thin stone heads found in Mexico and Guatemala. Archaeologist Steve Mitchell (1980) determined that the mounds of clam shells at the Pigeon Creek site on San Salvador were gathered during solstices which probably occasioned festivals. To indigenous cultures all living things and places were sacred.

The Taíno saw themselves as part of nature, not separate from it.

They knew which plants to use to cure ailments.

In cooking they wasted little; all parts of fishes and animals were cut or ground up and cooked in a pot with spices and served with a hot pepper condiment *(ají)*. Out of fish and animal bones, people fashioned spear darts, knives, scrapers, spoons, hoes and fish hooks. They used stingray spines for darts, barracuda and shark teeth for spear and arrow heads. They made sacks out of *iguana* skin.

The canoe played a fundamental role in their life. The Taíno canoe, *(canoa)* was hand-hewn from a solid log and fashioned in all sizes. Some could hold up to forty people. Their flat, thick bottoms took the waves well and once overturned were easily righted. The Taíno bailed out excess water with calabashes. Both canoe and wide oars were

crafted for swiftness and maneuverability. Canoes were used for reef fishing and trading. Taíno traded actively and rowed long distances. They tamed parrots and used them for trade. A ceremonial bottle found at Abaco (Lucayoneque) is made of clay found in North Florida. The jadeite and serpentine material used to make ceremonial celts found in many of the Bahama Islands may come from as far away as Guatemala. Cotton was an important trade product, as were stone pestles and other utilitarian items.

Lucayan Taíno pottery, called Palmetto Ware, is reddish in color. Because the Bahamian clay was inferior to the Antillean, it was tempered with bits of shell. Decorations appeared as mat marking, incised and punctated patterns. Their pottery is

not as decorative as Taínan pottery of the Dominican Republic or Haiti. However, their artistry is evident in their ornaments. A tiny flat bead, made from a conch shell, was found by Mary Jane Berman at the Three Dog Site on San Salvador. A needle-thin hole had been worked into the perfectly round bead, obviously the work of an artisan.

Archaeologist Theodoor De Booy (1913) found a linked cross or swastika pattern on pottery unearthed in the Caicos Islands in the early part of the 20th century. It was the Oriental and Native American design which according to Colonel Churchward is an ancient symbol of the four builders of the universe bringing order out of chaos.

The Nazi version moves in the opposite direction and represents destruction rather than creativity.

The Taíno believed that the sun was the great fire, the life force, the author of nature. The moon was the night sun, the mother goddess, the water goddess. Ritual dance *(Areíto)* lasted through the night and sometimes for days. On special ceremonial occasions the son of the *cacique* would recite the history of the king and his people.

The east was the great creative source. The Taíno thought Columbus' men were children of the sun, the dawn, the light, because they came from the east, the home of their ancestors. The Spanish cross was the symbol of the Christian religion, not the four great forces of creation, not the connectedness of all things. They exchanged gifts in friendship while Spaniards planted the cross to claim Guanahaní for the King and Queen of Spain, and renamed the island San Salvador (Holy Savior).

Las Casas wrote that there is no greater crime than that which is done under the mask of religion. He detailed the devastation of the Indies which followed in the wake of Columbus and speculated that if no gold had been found, colonization might have been a different story. Although he treated the Taíno well, Columbus condoned slavery because he thought the people had no religion. However, since they gave their gold as freely as gourds of water, Columbus tried to protect them. He wrote to the King and Queen that, "No one who is not a Christian should come to these parts." Only Christians came, but they came to steal, to enslave, to torture and to murder.

Greed festers at the root of this devastation. The Spaniards came for gold. They found it on Hispaniola, but not in the Lucayan Islands. King Ferdinand called them "the useless islands" and authorized raiding parties resulting in the enslavement and death of millions of Taíno. Blessing Their Majesties' endeavors was Rodrigo Borgia, Pope Alexander VI, a corrupt ecclesiastical politician. The Taíno embodied Plato's theory of unconditional love. They practiced what Joseph Campbell called "true religion," wherein you "love your enemies because they are the instruments of your destiny."

Explanation of Symbols

Colonel James Churchward spent fifty years piecing together the symbology that connected all humankind. He found its wellspring in the sacred writings of an ancient civilization on the continent of Mu (Lemuria), now submerged, but 70,000 years ago located in the Pacific Ocean. Churchward states that legends are oral history passed down. They reappear in the Orient and Babylon, in the Nascal tablets (Burma and India), on stone tablets found in Mexico and Peru, as pictographs in North America from British Columbia down through the America's Southwest, in the writings of the Greeks who studied in Egypt.

In *The Sacred Symbols of Mu* (one of three volumes) Chruchward gives the origin and original meanings of the symbols.

Symbols painted by the Woman on the Man's body:

The Butterfly — Ancient concept of law and order carried throughout the universe by the butterfly. The elongated circle is the universe, space without end. The face is a circle which represents the Creator and the four small circles in the face represent the Sacred Four (Winds, Directions, Forces of Creation). Together they number five which is the number of the full Godhead. The two antennae represent law and order. In the wing the five bars symbolize the Godhead and the four spaces between the Sacred Four. The tongue, the symbol of speech, carries the Creator's command that law and order be established throughout the universe.

The Circle — Monotheistic symbol of the Deity. It is the sun symbol of the Infinite One.

The Square — Symbol of the earth, the cardinal points, the four corners, the Four Great Primary Forces. According to D. G. Brinton (*Myths of the New World*, 1896), the number four was a sacred number to the pre-Columbian peoples of North America, South America and the Caribbean.

The Triangle — Represents the Triune Godhead and the Heaven where the Creator dwells.

The Spiral — Going to somewhere.  Coming from somewhere.

 *The Simple Cross* — Ancient symbol of the Sacred Four, the Four Great Primary Forces.

One right angle means builder. Shown here are the Four Great Builders of the universe.

The Snake — Symbolizes water, the beginning of life and the power of creation. An adorned serpent is a popular ancient symbol for the Deity as Creator or the creative attribute of the Godhead. The seven-headed snake symbolizes the seven stages of creation, the Seven Great Commands of Creation.

In the ancient writings of the Hindus, Babylonians and Egyptians these symbols read:

The Creator is one.  He is two in one.

These two produced a son or man.

According to Lao Tzu (Chinese philosopher 600 B.C.), these symbols read:

The Creator made one.  One became two.

Two produced three and so on.

The androgynous quality of the first being is discussed by Plato. In "Symposium," Plato states that man and woman were created combined in one body with four arms and four legs. The same androgyny appears symbolically in the Taíno legend of the creation of woman. The men were without women and one day they found snake-like creatures with arms and legs. The men decided to make these phallic creatures women by tying a woodpecker to each one. The bird, thinking the creature a stick of wood, bore a hole which became the female part.

In her book *Signs of Life* (1992), Angeles Arrien, through her study of ancient sources, discusses five basic universal shapes that appear in the art of all cultures throughout the world. She states that people of different cultures have similar meanings for these symbols. They are the circle (wholeness), the square (stability), the triangle (goals, dreams and visions), the equidistant cross (relationship) and the spiral (growth and change).

Regarding the places referred to in the "Songs of the Full Sun," descriptive phrases are used for proper names.

   The Land of the Sun is Mu.
*The Great Lake is the ancient Amazon which became the Great River.
   The Great South Land is South America.
   The Black River is the Negro River in South America.
   The Gentle Flowing River is the Orinoco in South America.
   The Great Land in the Western Ocean is Atlantis.
   The Western Ocean is the Atlantic.
   The Eastern Ocean is the Pacific.
   The City of Gold is Manoa, ancient city in South America.
   The North Sea is the Caribbean.

---

* On a map of South America, drawn in 1930, James Churchward labels the Amazon a "Sea" (*The Children of Mu,* p22).

An interesting connection appears in the report by Antonio Nuñez Jimenez, leader of the 1988 scientific expedition by canoe. While working in South America along the Amazon River, geologists made a significant observation. Jimenez reports that "In Pijuayal we discovered a bed of marine fossils, demonstrating that today's region where the Amazon flows was previously a shallow sea and in the case of Pijuayal, it constitutes a beach where sediment and marine remains originated. An important fact in the geological history of the Amazon."

Christopher Columbus used this symbol on his sketch of Hispaniola to indicate north. This sketch is the only surviving example of Columbus' cartography. All the journal entries in the novella are signed in Columbus' Spanish name - Cristóbal Colón.

Glossary of Taíno Words

Author's Note:

Dr. D. G. Brinton, writing in the last quarter of the 19th century, believed that the Arawak stock of languages was probably the most widely disseminated of any in South America, extending from the headwaters of the Paraguay River up to the northern coast and concentrated on the Orinoco River. Arawak speakers inhabited both the Lesser and Greater Antilles and the Bahamas, which brought the language within a short distance of the mainland of North America. His papers included the stories of the people compiled by Friar Ramón Pané at Columbus' request. Some are included in the novella. Brinton relied on two early 16th century Spanish historians and linguists close to the people. Bartolomé de las Casas, missionary in Hispaniola for forty years, knew the Taíno to be gentle and noble. Peter Martyr, never came to America but spoke to the Taíno brought to Spain by Columbus. Martyr found the language soft, "rich in vowels and pleasant to the ear" and an idiom "simple, sweet and sonorous."

The University of Miami's Special Collections permitted access and use of the two rare dictionaries of Bachiller (1888) and Zayas (1914). The author thanks Barbara Magnanini and Anubis Perez for their translations of the difficult Spanish.

AITI: The people had two names for the island Columbus named Hispaniola: Aití and Kiskeya (Quisqueya) which signified hope and a great land. Kiskeya means whole earth, lush and mountainous. The sacred cave from which all creation sprang was located on this island. Today the island is divided into two parts, Haiti and the Dominican Republic.

AJE: Also *hahe* (Granberry 2004). The sweet potato.

AJI: Also *axí*. A hot pepper condiment. Las Casas said that the people of America used it on everything they ate, whether the food was roasted or boiled or raw. The Spaniards considered it healthy because the inhabitants, who were moderate in the use of "dangerous things" in their diet, used so much of this condiment.

ANACAONA: Her name is formed from *ana* meaning flower and *caona* meaning gold, flower of gold. She was sister to King Behechio and wife of King Caonabó. After their deaths, she ruled as *cacique* of the territory of Xaraguá and Maguana.

According to Zayas (1914), when her brother died, Anacaona asked his wife, who was considered the most beautiful woman in all of Aití, to bury herself alive with her husband. It was the custom in Aití that the most beautiful and most loved woman of the chief should be buried alive with her dead husband.

Anacaona's people held her in high esteem for her poetic talent and great virtue. Columbus' brother Bartholomew called her "the fairest of the fair." Las Casas knew her and said, "She was a noteworthy woman, very prudent, very gracious, of great facility of speech and a good friend to the Christians." On the pretext of repaying Anacaona for her many favors to the Spaniards, Ovando, tyrannical governor of Aití, went to Xaraguá with seven hundred infantry and seventy horse. Anacaona and three hundred of her nobles welcomed Ovando with festivities, dances and songs as was the custom. Anacaona composed an *areíto* (historical romance) for the occasion. Three hundred women danced before the Spanish nobles. Ovando formulated a diabolical plot while he was honored for many days with the greatest simplicity and kindness. Telling Anacaona that he desired to show her nobles a cavalry charge in the European style, he surrounded the town, closing off all avenues of escape. He burned Anacaona's house, the village and all the people. He took Anacaona to Santo Domingo in chains and hanged her "in the presence of her people, who adored her."

AREITO: Also *areíte* (Granberry 2004). A traditional song and ritual dance. The people gave themselves passionately to dancing and thought of it as an occupation. Usually they formed circles. Sometimes the men and women danced separately, and at other times they danced together, each with the arms on the shoulders of the two adjacent people. They danced to their own singing, following the rhythm and mood of the *tekina* or leader who could be a man or a woman. They drank a wine made from fermented corn.

Lyrics sometimes referred to the mythology and traditions of their people, included the genealogies of their chiefs or described events in their daily lives. Since they had no written language, they kept their history alive by reciting events of the past. Among the famous *areítos* mentioned by Zayas are the ones written by Anacaona for the visit of the Spaniards to her dominions in Xaraguá. Ironically, the five-line fragment Zayas quotes in his dictionary contains Anacaona's name; one phrase can be translated to read "let's be free."

ATABEY: Also Atabex, Atabeira (Pané 1999. Notes by Arrom). Mother of Yúcahu "conceived without male intervention" (p4, n4). According to Pané, the Taíno had five names for Atabey which some scholars thought were aspects of the Mother Goddess. One was Atabeira (*beira* means "water"). "A free translation…more attentive to their sacred character than to their literal meaning, would read thus: Mother of the Waters; Lady of the Moon, the Tides, and Maternity; Universal Mother" (p4, n5). In the novella and film, Atabeira is Mother Ocean and Atabey is the All Mother.

BAHAMA: The island of Grand Bahama. Today the Lucayan Islands are called the Bahamas.

BANANA: A species of plantain. The naturalist, Oviedo, thought that the banana was brought to the Caribbean from Spain. Other Spanish historians disagree and say that various species of the fruit are indigenous.

BARBACOA: The word means grilled meat. It was also a raised place used to store corn safely. According to Rouse 1992, the English word barbecue "originated among the Taínos," but was "a later acquisition." "It appears to have been carried to the United Stated by French speakers after they replaced the Taínos in Haiti" (p171).

BEHECHIO: King of the province of Xaraguá in Aití and brother of Anacaona. Among his subjects, Behechio had thirty-two *caciques* and thirty wives. Guanahata was his favorite wife.

BEHIKE: *Behike* is the common name for shaman, holy man and healer. In the novella, the character called Father is a *behike*.

BIAYA: The flamingo, a long-legged, pink-feathered bird. The people would run after them, catch them and make a broth the color of saffron. The Spaniards found the meat as tasty as pheasant.

BIJA: The plant called *achiote* is used today in Mexico and islands of the Greater Antilles as a condiment. It is a small bush and the flowers come in bunches. The seeds are found in compartments inside a hairy pod about the size and shape of an almond as it appears on the tree. The seeds are sticky like tender wax. The people made balls with the seeds. To dye their skins red, they would rub these waxy balls on their faces and bodies. The dye had a strong odor and served as a mosquito repellent. The botanical name is *Bixa orellana*.

BIMINI: (The Twins) Two small islands in the Bahamas. The Taíno told Ponce de Leon that a magic spring was located there. He went in search of this fountain of youth, missed Bimini, but found Florida.

BOHIO: Also *bohi* - house (Granberry 2004). Columbus' guide pointed in the direction of Aití and called it Bohío which is the generic name for their living quarters. Since their ancestors came from Aití, the Lucayan Taíno guide may have used the word to mean homeland or ancestral home. Las Casas described their houses in Aití as round, made of sticks and straw (probably palm thatch) with bell-shaped roofs. There was a hole in the center of the roof to let the smoke out. Their houses were clean and the larger ones "so pleasant that an emperor could live in one."

BORIKEN: Also Borinquen. The island of Puerto Rico. Granberry 2004 states that Puerto Rico "with 20 chiefdoms or provinces, had, for all practical purposes, been organized into a single confederated kingdom, Borinquen, the People's Homeland" (p9). Columbus arrived there in November 1493. Zayas says that an old Spanish encyclopedia states the name means the land of the valiant, but the book did not say where that definition originated. Bieke is the little island very near the eastern end of Puerto Rico. Today it is called Vieques.

CACIQUE: Also *kasike* (Granberry 2004). Chief or leader of a tribe. A woman could also receive this distinction among her people.

CAICOS: (North Caicos) It is also the name of the group of islands southeast of the Bahama chain. Geographically, they are considered part of the Bahama group. The Spaniards noted that these islands lie very close to the water and thought them dangerous to navigation.

CANOA: The Taíno *canoa* was flat-bottomed, hand-hewn from a single tree trunk and could carry from one up to 150 people. These vessels were capable of the tremendous speed and maneuverability necessary for traders to cover the long distances between islands. The *canoa* was long and narrow. The six-inch-thick flat bottom prevented capsizing. If a *canoa* filled with water in a rain storm, the people bailed it out with calabashes. Columbus noted that the paddle resembled a "baker's peel" and was narrow at the tip to cut the water. The people filed their oars with the rough skin of a man-eating shark. The *canoa* can turn 360 degrees; the rower at the stern acts as a rudder.

CAONABO: The Golden One. Since he was *cacique* of Maguana in Aití, the province was sometimes called the "golden house or place where gold is abundant." Granberry references Las Casas as saying that Caonabó was a "native of the Lucayan Islands." After his death, his wife, Anacaona succeeded him as ruler of Maguana.

Caonabó was the first Taíno to fight against the Spanish invaders. Columbus' vessel, the *Santa María*, was wrecked at Cape Hatien on Christmas Day 1492 and he was forced to establish a fort there called Navidad. He left behind thirty-nine men and when a few of them wandered into Caonabó's territory, they were killed. The *cacique* then marched on the fort, killing all the Spaniards and burning the village. Later, Caonabó's ten thousand men attacked another fort. But, even with his superior numbers, he was forced to retreat; his arms did not equal those of the Spaniards.

Columbus offered this humorous strategy to capture Caonabó. Somehow the *cacique* must be trapped and forced to put clothes on, so that if he should run away, a soldier might have something to grab. The agile soldier Alonso de Hojeda apprehended Caonabó. Although he was very capable of doing so, Hojeda did not have to chase the *cacique*.

The Taíno people loved the shine of the brass and steel used by the Spaniards. Their word *turé* means sky. One of the reasons the people thought the Spaniards came from the sky was their shiny adornments. Hojeda invited Caonabó to make peace and promised the *cacique* a prize. When Caonabó arrived, Hojeda produced manacles made of shining steel—metals from Vizcaya engraved with the arms of the kings of Castile. The conquistador offered to dress Caonabó's wrists and feet with ornaments in the same manner that the king would wear them. Of course, the *cacique* could not refuse such a precious gift. Once chained, Caonabó was imprisoned in the hold of a galleon for several months. A storm came up before the ship could set sail for Spain; Caonabó and six hundred men drowned. The Spaniards established a town where Caonabó was captured. It was called the Villa of San Juan de la Maguana.

CASABE: Also *cassabe, cassava* and *manioc*. The bread made from the *yuca* tuber and the staple food of the Taíno. Sometimes the bread was dipped in water seasoned with *ají*. Las Casas writes that the women made the bread and as they grated the root, they "sang a song that had a nice tune."

A poisonous juice had to be extracted from the grated flour before the bread-making process could continue. Some Taíno, weary of their enslavement in the mines of Aití, drank this juice as one form of suicide.

CAYACOA: King of the Higuey. His widow was baptized Dona Inez de Cayacoa.

CEIBA: A large tree used for making canoes. Its trunk is thick and its branches strong. Brinton states that the people considered the tree sacred because its limbs stretched to the four winds and its roots dug into the waters. The *ceiba* blooms every four years and inside these capsules a soft silky material wraps the seeds. Today the *ceiba* is commonly called the silk cottonwood tree. The mahogany is another tree used to make canoes. Sometimes tree trunks measure thirty feet high and twelve feet in diameter. The botanical name is *Swietenia mahogani*. In the islands today the mahogany tree is called madeira which is like the Spanish word for wood *(madera)*. Cedar is another wood used for canoes. It grew along the coasts of Puerto Rico and was considered sacred.

CEMI: Also *semí* and *zemí*. A sacred image of wood or stone made in the likeness of a human figure, an animal or a vegetable. Some had special faculties. A *cemí* might be used to bring rain or to assist in childbirth. The three pointed stones, usually the representation of Yúcahu, the Great Deity, were buried in the earth to help the crops grow.

The Taíno carved personal images and wore them for protection. According to Dr. Julian Granberry's linguistic study, the word means spirit.

COCO: The fruit called the coconut. Historians and archaeologists debate whether the coconut is indigenous to the islands of the Caribbean. The Spanish lexicographer, Zayas (1914), remarks that the coconut was found in a wild state on islands and cays in the Caribbean in the early 1500s and it had industrial uses. According to Zayas, the word is of Greek origin. The Greek word *koyki* describes this plant.

COHOBA: Name of the plant and the ceremony. The Taíno crushed the beans from the seed pod and inhaled the powder to produce a narcotic effect.

Las Casas writes that herbal powders the color of cinnamon were placed in a smooth, black shiny bowl as beautiful as gold or silver. The instrument for sniffing the powder was hollow and forked and made from the same wood. The forked end was placed in the nostrils and the single tube in the bowl.

At the *cohoba* ceremony the people would sit and discuss important issues and speak to the *cemí* to get answers to their questions. Las Casas noted that the effect produced was like being intoxicated and at times the people seemed to lose their senses and consciousness. The Taíno said they sometimes went into a trance state where they saw "a thousand visions."

CUBA: One of the islands in the Greater Antilles. Columbus died thinking that Cuba was mainland China. Morison writes, "Las Casas has a plausible explanation of how the Admiral was misled by his helpful hosts. A district in the interior of Cuba where a limited quantity of gold existed was called by the people Cubanacan (mid-Cuba). Whenever Columbus produced a gold object and asked where more could be found, they pronounced this word, which he mistook for "El Gran Can" (Morison, 1942 p257).

CUBAGUA: An island near Margarita off the northeastern part of Venezuela, South America famous for its pearl beds. The Lucayan Taíno were not suited for the plantations or the gold and silver mines of Aití. However, they were excellent swimmers and although the going price for slaves was four pesos, the Spaniards sold the Lucayans for 150 gold pesos each.

In his book *The Devastation of the Indies: a Brief Account*, Las Casas relates the excruciating experience of the Lucayans at Cubagua:

> The pearl fishers dive into the sea at a depth of five fathoms (thirty feet), and do this from sunrise to sunset, and remain for many minutes without breathing, tearing the oysters out of their rocky beds where the pearls are formed. They come to the surface with a netted bag of these oysters where a Spanish torturer is waiting in a canoe, and if the pearl diver shows signs of wanting to rest, he is showered with blows...

Often a pearl diver does not return to the surface, for these waters are infested with man-eating sharks...that can kill, eat, and swallow a whole man...And in this extraordinary labor, or better put, in this infernal labor, the Lucayans are finally consumed...

Ironically, the word Cubagua means "without water."

DUHO: Also *duhu* (Granberry 2004). A ceremonial seat made of wood or stone carved in images both anthropomorphic and zoomorphic. Often the ears and eyes of the animals were made of gold.

GUACANAGARI: King of Marién in Aití, situated in the area of Cape Hatien where the *Santa María* was wrecked on Christmas Day 1492. Guacanagarí and his people helped Columbus salvage his supplies from the vessel before it broke up on the reef. The *cacique* took Columbus to his village and gave him two of his best houses. Columbus established the first Spanish settlement in America there and called it La Navidad. The Admiral left behind thirty-nine men to garrison his new fort. When he returned eleven months later, the men had been killed and the village burned.

The depraved conduct of the Spaniards brought the wrath of the people. Caonabó and his men destroyed the fort. Guacanagarí claimed to have fought on the side of the Spaniards. Always on the side of the Taíno, Las Casas considered him a traitor to his country.

GUAHABA: Province in Aití ruled by chief Hatuey.

GUANAHANI: The Lucayan island Columbus first sighted, made landfall and named San Salvador.

GUANIMA: Zayas identifies this island as Eleuthera in the Bahamas. According to the Turin map, circa 1523, Guanima is Cat Island and Ziguateo is Eleuthera. Granberry gives the name as Sibateo "Distant Rocky Place."

GUARIONEX: King of Maguá in Aití. Guarionex was apprehended along with fourteen other *caciques* who led an insurrection against the Spaniards. Only two *caciques* were punished. Guarionex and the others were released. In return for this gesture of good will, the Spaniards had peace, but only for a few days. The people attacked again. When Columbus returned to Aití, he sent his brother to quiet the rebellion. Six thousand naked people painted in various colors, but with little weaponry, were forced by the Spaniards to retreat to the woods where they were soon captured. Guarionex was chained in the same ship with Caonabó. A hurricane sank the vessel in the port at Santo Domingo. Everyone died.

GUAYABA: The fruit that in English is called Guava. Oviedo thought the tree, with its hard resistant wood, was pretty and the bloom fragrant. The leaves were used to smoke meat. It is a sacred fruit. The spirits of the dead became owls at night to feast on *guayaba*.

HAMACA: A hammock. The Taíno used it for sleeping and for transporting their chiefs from one place to another. Hammocks were fashioned from ropes made from the fiber of the agave plant.

HAOMATE: Crooked Island (Granberry 2004).

HATUEY: *Cacique* of Guahába in Aití. He escaped after Anacaona was hanged and fled to Cuba to warn the people about the Spanish. He organized a resistance to fight Diego Veláquez who was beginning to occupy Cuba.

Thinking that gold was the god of the Spaniards, he ordered all the gold to be thrown in the river. Then he and his people sang and danced an *areíto* in the hope of appeasing this god. Their prayers were futile. Hatuey sent the women and children into the hills and attacked the Spaniards whose superior arms, once again, vanquished his warriors.

Hatuey was burned at the stake. Las Casas writes that when the Franciscan friar in attendance asked Hatuey to accept the religion of the Spaniards so he would go to heaven and avoid the fires of hell, Hatuey replied that if the Spaniards went to this heaven, he preferred to go to the other place. Elderly Cubans, who know the story, like to believe that Hatuey also said, "This land will never be free." Certainly he is the champion of the oppressed peoples of the Caribbean countries.

HIGUEY: Territory ruled by King Cayacoa. The people of this province were warlike. They used poison arrows like the Caribs, who, by 1470 had occupied much of Samana, the peninsula just above this province in Aití.

HIWAKA: Parrot. (Granberry 2004).

HURACAN: A storm with strong winds. According to Brinton, Huracán means the Great Breath and was thought of as a creative force that was considered the heart of the sky.

HUTIA: The *hutía* is a small quadruped found in the islands of the Caribbean and the Bahamas. A staple food for the Lucayan Taíno, it is almost extinct today.

IGUANA: A reptile of great size with an indented crest running from its head down its back. The animal is fierce-looking, but quite harmless. Oviedo says that the "animal is better to eat than to see. Very few people who have seen it have dared to eat it." The white meat had a delicate flavor which the Spaniards loved.

INAGUA: One of the islands in the Bahamas which provides a natural reserve for the flamingo. Granberry translates the meaning of the Taíno name for the island as

"The Small Eastern Land," which may mean that the people came from Cuba into the Bahamas (2004, p82).

JAMAICA: It is one of the four major islands in the Greater Antilles. Its name means land of abundant springs.

LUCAYONEQUE: (Great Abaco) According to Granberry the Taíno name means "The People's Distant Waters Land" (2004, p83). Great and Little Abaco Islands form the main of Abaco and together with the surrounding cays, the group is called the Abacos.

MAGUA: Province in Aití governed by the *cacique* Guarionex. The Spanish named this territory La Vega Real which describes a low land which is flat and fertile.

MAGUANA: Province in Aití ruled by Caonabó. Its fertile land is both beautiful and healthy.

MAIZ: The corn of the Americas. It was abundant everywhere, even in Florida. The native people cooked it in water, then ground it and roasted the grains wrapped in corn leaves.

MANATI: An aquatic mammal of great size which eats grass near the banks of rivers. It is commonly called a sea cow and has thick skin like a whale and no scales. Columbus thought they were mermaids. The Spaniards ate the *manatí* on Fridays and could believe they were eating meat. To them, it tasted like good veal.

Las Casas tells a story of a domesticated *manatí* called Mato which means magnificent. The *cacique* Caramateji caught a young *manatí*, raised it and kept it twenty-six years in the river which ran by his village. Mato was so tame and so friendly he would come out of the water and play with the children and eat in people's houses. His size and strength enabled him to ferry ten people at a time across the river. They loved to play with him and Mato especially enjoyed it when the people sang.

One day a Spaniard came to the village to see if Mato's skin was as thick as people said it was. He called to Mato and when the *manatí* came out of the water, he threw a spear at him. Although Mato was not wounded physically, his feelings were hurt. After that time, he would not come out of the water if there was a clothed, bearded man about, even if he were called. One year the River Atibonico rose so high that the currents carried Mato the Magnificent out to sea, which saddened Caramateji and his subjects.

MARIEN: The province in Aití governed by Guacanagarí. In his village Columbus established his first settlement. In writing about Marién, Zayas (1914) says that from the mountains to the sea, gracious and happy rivers descend and the valleys have good land for cultivation. There were mines of copper in the mountains. In these days of Spanish occupation, one gold peso could buy one pound of copper.

MATININO: Ramón Pané reported that the people had told Columbus of an island that had much gold and only women. The men visited once a year for breeding purposes. The female children were allowed to remain on the island, but the male children were sent to the island of men. In this respect the Taíno story is similar to the Greek myth of the Amazons. In spite of the lure of gold, Columbus never went to this island. Historian Martin Fernandez de Navarette thought Matininó was St. Lucia. Washington Irving thought it was Martinique. However, the Island Caribs knew Martinique as Ionacaera. In the late 16th century a Spanish document stated an island named Martininó was one of the Lucayan Islands. José Juan Arrom, the editor of the new edition of Pané's *Account* thinks "that Matininó is a mythical landscape and not a geographical location" (1999, p7, n20).

MAYAGUANA: One of the Lucayan Islands. Granberry states that Mayaguana means "Lesser Midwestern Land," which supports the theory that the island may have been settled by people from Aití (2004, p83 & p85).

PAPAYA: The plant has a straight trunk with only a few palm-like leaves at the top. Its fruit is considered medicinal and is applied to stomach ailments. The botanical name is *Carica papaya*. Today, Bahamians call it papaw.

SAMANA: One of the Bahamas. According to the Juan de la Cosa map of 1500, Samana is Long Island. It is south of Guanahaní and considered to be Columbus' island of landfall by Joseph Judge (1986). Granberry states that the Taíno name means "Small Middle Forest" (2004, p83).

SAOMETE: Crooked/Fortune/Acklins. Keegan states that in his quest for gold, Columbus sailed from Guanahaní (San Salvador) to Rum Cay (Santa María de la Conceptíon), Long Island (Fernandina), then to Crooked Island, which his captives called Saomete and he renamed La Isabela. There Columbus spent three days seeking an audience with "the king who had much gold" before giving up and sailing to Cuba. In his study of Columbus' journals, Keegan finds four different spellings for the Taíno name Saomete. "Columbus may have been confused by the use of one name for both the island and the village of the paramount chief. Alternatively, two similar names with slight difference in word endings or in pronunciation might have been used…Samaot (Samoet) may refer to the village of the chief, while Saomete (Saometo) refers to the island(s) on which the settlement was located…" Refer to Keegan (1992, pgs196-198 & p199) for his map of Crooked and Acklins islands, including Lucayan site locations.

TABACO: Las Casas writes that the Taíno would tightly roll the leaves of this plant and smoke it. Sometimes the leaves were crushed and mixed with other herbs for medicinal purposes. In Arabic it is called *tabbaq*.

TAINO: The word means good or noble.

TAINOTI: Also *Taíno Tí*. A Taíno greeting meaning "I honor the spirit within you. We are one." The Lakota phrase *Mitakuye Oyasin* means "all my relations" or "we are all related." In a village near Ucluelet in British Columbia, Canada, there is a Nuu-chah-nulth expression *Hishuk ish ts'awak* which means "everything is one." All these expressions suggest that everything physical and spiritual is connected.

TEKINA: Also *Tequina*. A master or leader. The word is also applied to any man or woman cunning in any science: fishers, fowlers, hunters and makers of nets.

XARAGUA: Province in Aití governed first by Behechio then by his sister Anacaona. According to Loven, (1979) the province grew a fine quality cotton. The manners and customs of the people of Xaraguá were refined and their speech aristocratic.

YUCA: The tuber used to make the bread called *cassabe*. *Yucubia (Manioc esculenta)* is the plant source.

YUCAHU: The Lord of the Yuca. "Las Casas paraphrases Pané's text as follows: 'the people of this island Hispaniola had a certain faith in and knowledge of a one and true God, who was immortal and invisible, for none could see him, who had no beginning, whose dwelling place and residence is heaven'" (Pané, notes by Arrom 1999, p31, n132 & pgs 3 & 4, n3). Indigenous cultures have various names for the One who plays a pivotal role in their spiritual lives: the Unseen Spirit, the Creator, and in some Native American cultures this figure is referred to as the Great Mystery.

Hatuey Ascending →

Note on the painting by the artist Alton Lowe
Hatuey is standing in the center of a blood-red cross draped over the earth. Painted on his chest is the equidistant cross in motion symbolizing the creation of the world and the connectedness of everything and everyone on it. The lower part of his body is darker, more earthy, grounded. As Hatuey passes through the stormy clouds of the conquest and lifts up into the light of the heavens, more light appears on his upper body. I felt peaceful in my mind and as I painted the aura, I saw rainbows flashing around Hatuey's body. During the flow of the final painting process, I could not stop and I did not stop.

Bibliography for Macmillan Edition 1991

Adams, Beatrice Wolper
    1975   *Horticulture of San Salvador Island.* San Salvador, Bahamas: New World Museum Publication.

Bachiller y Morales, Don Antonio
    1883   *Cuba Primitiva: Origen, Lenguas, Tradiciones e Historia de los Indios de las Antillas Mayores y las Lucayas.* Habana.

Berman, Mary Jane
    1988   Personal Interview. 12 June.

Bierhorst, John, ed.
    1976   *The Red Swan: Myths and Tales of the American Indians.* New York: Farrar, Strauss and Giroux.

Bourne, Edward Gaylord
    1906   Columbus, Ramón Pané and the Beginnings of American Anthropology. *Proceedings of the American Antiquarian Society* 17: 310-348.

Brinton, Daniel
    1871   The Arawack Language of Guiana in its Linguistic and Ethnological Relations. *Transactions of the American Philosophical Society* (London) 14: 427-444.

    1890   *Essays of an Americanist.* Philadelphia: David McKay.

    1896   *The Myths of the New World.* Philadelphia: David McKay.

Brown, Tom Jr., with Brandt Morgan
    1983   *Tom Brown's Field Guide to Wilderness Survival.* New York: Berkley Books.

Campbell, David
    1978   *The Ephemeral Islands: A Natural History of the Bahamas.* London: Macmillan Caribbean.

Campbell, Joseph with Bill Moyers
    1988   *The Power of Myth.* Edited by Betty Sue Flowers. New York: Doubleday.

Carr, Robert S. and Sandra Riley
    1982   An Effigy Ceramic Bottle from Green Turtle Cay, Abaco. *The Florida Anthropologist* 35: 200-202.

Churchward, Col. James
    1988   *The Children of Mu.* Albuquerque: BE Books.

    1987   *The Lost Continent of Mu.* Albuquerque: BE Books.

    1988   *The Sacred Symbols of Mu.* Albuquerque: BE Books.

Curry, Robert A.
    1928   *Bahamian Lore.* Paris: Printed Privately.

De Booy, Theodoor
    1913   Lucayan Artifacts from the Bahamas. *American Anthropologist* 15: 1-7.

Donnelly, Ignatius
    1882   *Atlantis: The Antediluvian World.* New York: Dover Publications, Inc. 1976.

Drummond, Lee
    1981   The Serpent's Children: Semiotics of Cultural Genesis in Arawak and Trobiand Myth. *American Ethnologist* 8: 633-60.

    1977   Structure and Process in the Interpretation of South America Myth: The Arawak Dog Spirit People. *American Anthropologist* 79: 842-868.

Eden, Richard, trans.
    1555   *The Decades of the Newe Worlde or West Indies.* By Pietro Martire d'Anghiera. London: NP.

Frye, John
    1973   *The Search for the Santa Maria.* New York: Dodd, Mead and Co.

Granberry, Julian M.
    1955   A Survey of Bahamian Archeology. M.A. Thesis, Department of Anthropology. Gainesville: University of Florida.

Hoffman, Charles
    1987   Archaeological Investigations at the Long Bay Site, San Salvador, Bahamas. *First San Salvador Conference: Columbus and His World.* Compiled by Donald T. Gerace. San Salvador: Bahamian Field Station. 237-245.

    1967   Bahama Prehistory: Cultural Adaptation to an Island Environment. Dissertation. University of Arizona.

    1970   The Palmetto Grove Site on San Salvador, Bahamas. *Contributions to the Florida State Museum.* Social Sciences, Number 16: 1-26. Gainesville: University of Florida.

Jimenez, Antonio Nuñez
 1988 Expedition by Canoe from the Amazon to the Caribbean.
   A talk delivered at a symposium at the Bahamian Field Station, San Salvador, Bahamas. 19-21 June.

Judge, Joseph
 1986 Where Columbus Found the New World. *National Geographic* 170: 566-572, 578-599.

Keegan, William F.
 1985 Horticulturists: Population and Expansion in the Prehistoric Bahamas. Dissertation. UCLA.

 1982 Lucayan Fishing: An Experimental Approach. *The Florida Anthropologist* 35: 146-161.

 1988 New Directions in Bahamian Archaeology. *Journal of the Bahamas Historical Society* 10: 3-8.

Krieger, Herbert W.
 1931 *Aboriginal Indian Pottery of the Dominican Republic.* U.S. National Museum Bulletin 156. Washington, D.C.: Smithsonian Institution.

Las Casas, Bartolomé de
 1974 *The Devastation of the Indies: A Brief Account.* Translated by Herma Briffault. New York: The Seabury Press.

 1971 *History of the Indies.* Translated and edited by Andrée Collard. New York: Harper and Row.

Leach, Edmond
 1961 Lévi Strauss in the Garden of Eden: An Examination of Some Recent Developments of the Analysis of Myth. *Transactions of the New York Academy of Sciences* 23: 386-396.

Loven, Sven
 1979 *Origins of the Tainan Culture, West Indies.* Göteborg 1935. USA: AMS, 1979.

Mitchell, Steven W.
 1980 Analysis of Tidal Growth Sequences in Populations of Codakia Orbicularis (Linnaeus) from the Lucayan Arawak Pigeon Creek Site, San Salvador. *Bahamas Archaeological Project Reports and Papers.* San Salvador, Bahamas: Bahamian Field Station, 1980: 1-20.

Montas, Borrell
 ND *Arte Taíno.* Santo Domingo: Central Bank of the Dominican Republic.

Morison, Samuel Eliot
    1942   *Admiral of the Ocean Sea: A Life of Christopher Columbus.* Boston: Little, Brown and Co.

Neihardt, John G.
    1959   *Black Elk Speaks.* New York: Pocket Books - Washington Square Press.

Ober, Frederick
    1894   Aborigines of the West Indies. *American Antiquarian Society* 9: 270-313.

Olsen, Fred
    1974   *On the Trail of the Arawaks.* Norman: University of Oklahoma Press.

Oviedo y Valdez, Gonzalo Fernández
    1959   *Natural History of the West Indies.* Translated and edited by Sterling A. Stoudemire. Chapel Hill: University of North Carolina Press.

Plato
    1952   Critias. *The Dialogues of Plato.* The Great Books. Vol. 7. Translated by Benjamin Jowett. Chicago: Encyclopaedia Britannica, Inc. 478-485.

    1950   Symposium *Dialogues of Plato.* The Jowett Translation. New York: Washington Square Press. 161-234.

Prescott, W. H.
    1909   *The Conquest of Mexico.* Vol. 1. New York: E. P. Dutton and Co. 2 Vols.

Priego, Joaquin R.
    1977   *Cultura Taina.* Santo Domingo: Publicaciones America.

Rose, Richard
    1987   Lucayan Lifeways at the Time of Columbus. *First San Salvador Conference: Columbus and His World.* Compiled by Donald T. Gerace. San Salvador: Bahamian Field Station. 321-339.

    1982   The Pigeon Creek Site, San Salvador, Bahamas. *The Florida Anthropologist* 35: 129-145.

Rouse, Irving
    1948   The Arawak and The Carib. *Smithsonian Bureau of American Ethnology Bulletin 143: Handbook of South American Indians.* Ed. Julian H. Stewart. 4: 522-545, 546-565.

    1982   The Olsen Collection from Ile á Vache, Haiti. *The Florida Anthropologist* 35: 169-185.

Saur, Carl
    966   *The Early Spanish Main.* Berkeley: U of California Press.

Sears, William H. and Shaun O. Sullivan
    1978   Bahamas Prehistory. *American Antiquity* 43: 3-25.

Smith, Rhea M.
    1933   Anthropology in Florida. *Florida Historical Society* 11: 151-172.

Spence, Lewis
    1974   *Atlantis Discovered.* New York: Causeway Books.

Statnekou, Daniel
    1987   *Animated Earth.* Berkeley, California: North Atlantic Books.

Tavares, Juan Tomas
    1976   *Los Indios de Quisqueya.* Santo Domingo: Editora de Santo Domingo.

Tedlock, Dennis, trans.
    1985   *Papal Yuh: The Mayan Book of the Dawn of Life.* New York: Simon and Schuster, Inc.

Winter, John
    1987   San Salvador in 1492: Its Geography and Ecology. *First San Salvador Conference: Columbus and His World.* Compiled by Donald T. Gerace. San Salvador: Bahamian Field Station. 313-320.

Zayas y Morales, Alfredo
    1914   *Lexicografía Antillana: Diccionario de Voces Usadas por los Aborígenes de las Antillas Mayores y de Algunas de las Menores y Consideraciones Acerca de su Significado y de su Formacion.* Habana.

Bibliography for Parrot House Edition 2012

Arrien, Angeles
    1992   *Signs of Life: The Five Universal Shapes and How To Use Them.* Sonoma, CA: Arcus Publishing Co.

Bercht, Fatima, Estella Brodsky, John Alan Farmer and Dicey Taylor, editors
    1997   *Taíno: Pre-Columbian Art and Culture from the Caribbean.* New York: El Museo Del Barrio, Monacelli Press.

Granberry, Julian & Gary S. Vescelius
    2004   *Languages of te Pre-Columbian Antilles.* Tuscaloosa: U of Alabama Press.

Keegan, William F.
    1992   *The People Who Discovered Columbus.* Gainesville: U of Florida Press.

Imhotep, David
    2012 *The First Americans Were Africans.* Bloomington, IN: Author House Press.

Las Casas, Bartolomé de
    1992 *In Defense of the Indies.* Translated by Stafford Poole, C.M. DeKalb: Northern Illinois University Press.

Leicester, L. Anthony, Sandra Riley and Chris McLaughlin.
    2007 *San Salvador: An Island Guide.* Williams & Co.

Mail, Thomas E.
    1997 *The Hopi Survival Kit.* New York: Penguin Books.

Mann, Charles C.
    2006 *1491: New Revelations of the Americas Before Columbus.* New York: Vintage, Random House.

Pané, Fray Ramón
    1999 *An Account of the Antiquities of the Indians.* A New Edition, with an Introductory Study, Notes & Appendixes: (Columbus, Martyr, Las Cases) by José Juan Arrom. Translated by Susan C. Griswold. Durham & London: Duke UP.

Rouse, Irving.
    1992 *The Taínos: Rise and Decline of the People Who Greeted Columbus.* New Haven & London: Yale University Press.

Sale, Kirkpatrick.
    1990 *The Conquest of Paradise: Christopher Columbus and the Columbian Legacy.* New York: Plume. A. Knopf.

Waters, Frank
    1977 *Book of the Hopi.* New York: Penguin Books.

Tracing Steps

The Bahamian children praying at the monument on San Salvador (placed through the efforts of Columbian scholar Ruth Wolper in 1965) symbolize hope for the future. Resting in the tranquil waters of Long Bay is a Taíno canoe, placed in the painting by the artist as a symbol. That canoe was named after the heroic Taíno *cacique*, Hatuey, who defied the Spaniards in Cuba. Equally singular was the canoe's journey to San Salvador in 1988. For all who greeted the *Hatuey* that day, the canoe remains a symbol of the spirit of indigenous peoples in the Bahamas, the Caribbean and everywhere in the world.

Prior to our encounter with the *Hatuey* on San Salvador in 1988, Alton and I had taken different roads before we found ourselves on the same path. Born in the Bahamas, Alton Lowe became an internationally acclaimed artist. His keen interest in history led him to create a museum on his native island of Green Turtle Cay, Abaco (GTC). On hiatus from theatre, I came to the Bahamas to work as a historical researcher for a development company on San Salvador. In 1980, I met Alton on GTC where he and James Mastin worked to create a Memorial Sculpture Garden dedicated to the descendants of the early settlers. Alton helped me research and publish my history of the Bahamas, *Homeward Bound,* and I wrote the text for James' sculptures in the Garden. When Alton was commissioned to create a series of paintings of the Lucayan Taíno for a stamp issue celebrating the Quincentennial, Postmaster General John Saunders sent us to San Salvador to research the project.

The Hatuey

As luck or destiny would have it, a multi-national scientific expedition led by Cuban scientist Dr. Antonio Núñez Jímenez arrived at San Salvador on 14 June 1988 (see map on pages viii-ix). Their 15 month 10,000 mile journey by canoe from the Amazon to the Caribbean had three objectives: to trace the route of the pre-Columbian island settlers, to conduct scientific research along the way and to take a concrete step toward Latin American and Caribbean unity. On 2 March 1987, the expedition left Quito with five canoes built by the Quichuas of Ecuador. Navigating through earthquake debris that filled the Napo River with tree trunks, they carried on through rain into the Amazon, along the Negro and Orinoco rivers into the punishing waves of the Caribbean Sea. The scientists (sociologists, ethnologists, botanists, geographers, archaeologists, zoologists, geophysicists) worked along the way and participated in symposiums with scientists of the host counties they visited. The US State Department would not allow the canoes to navigate the waters near the US Virgins and Puerto Rico. At the same time the news that the expedition was denied entrance to Puerto Rico, the *Hatuey* was capsized by rough seas. Without a permit to travel to Puerto Rico, the canoe drifted; carried by the wind it crashed over a dangerous reef. Defiant of protocol and with no visa, the *Hatuey* beached itself on the US Marine Corps firing range at Vieques. The fisherman who found it thought it a wounded whale. The people of Vieques saw it as a symbol of their cultural identity and dressed the canoe in flowers.

It was many months before the canoe could rejoin the Expedition. Once the *Hatuey* arrived on Sal Salvador, Don Gerace organized an impromptu symposium at the Bahamian Field Station and provided interpreters for the English and Spanish speakers.

He arranged receptions, informal gatherings and conversations with scientists and Bahamian officials and people of the island. The week was packed with a rich exchange of knowledge and friendship. Myrna Pagan of Vieques told us the story of the subsequent reunion of the canoe and the Expedition. Her son Pablo joined the crew for the final leg of the journey from Puerto Rico to San Salvador. When she recounted the suffering of her people living in the middle of the island between two military installations and her daughter awakened by the vibrations of the shelling, we cried. And when she spoke about the canoe, the *Hatuey* as a unifying symbol of the warrior who gave back the soul to the people, we cheered.

Photo by Alton Lowe

Back Row, left to right: *Don Gerace, Awinda Palau, Myrna Pagan Connelly, Aléjandro Hartman Matos, Antonio Núñez Jíménez, Consuelo Varela, Silvano Lora, Sandra Riley*
Front Row, left to right: *Crewman, Crewman, Gail Saunders, Davidson Hepburn, Michael Pablo Connelly Pagan, Crewman, Crewman.*

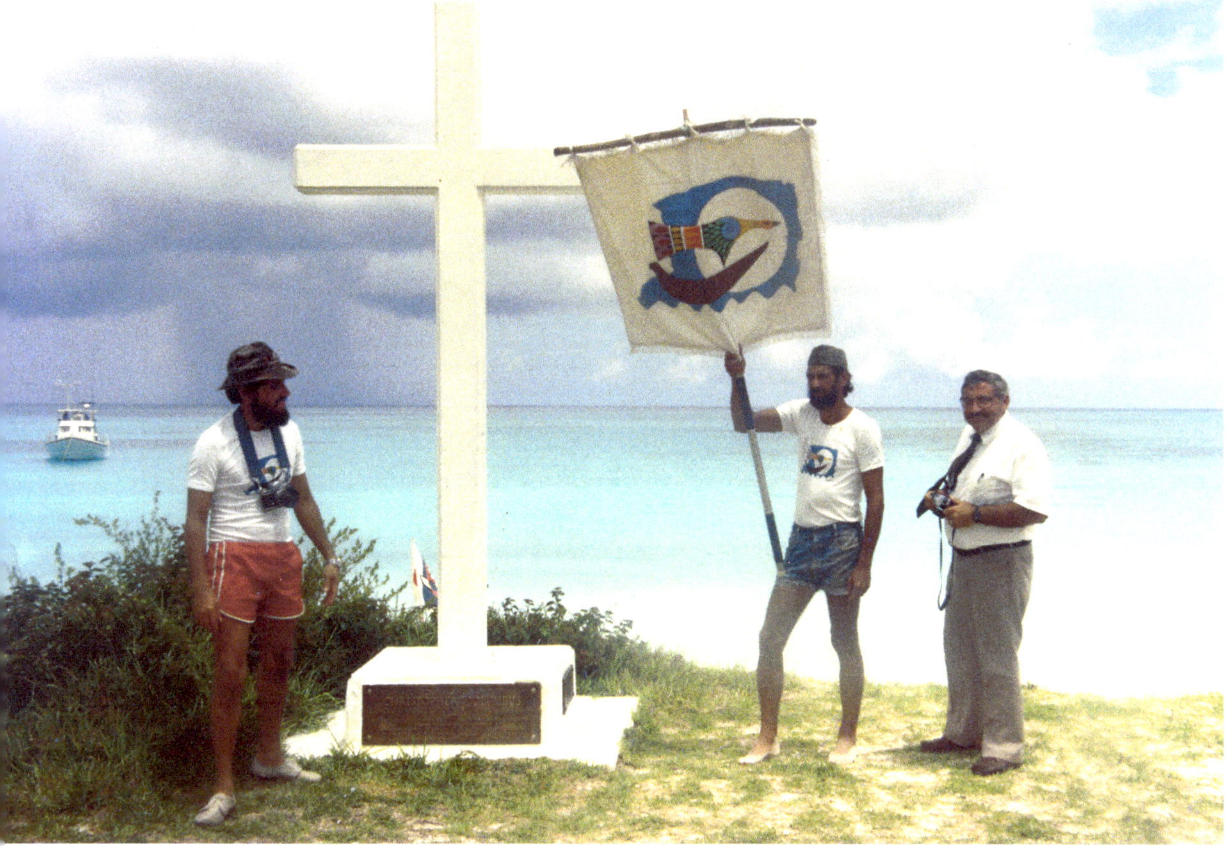

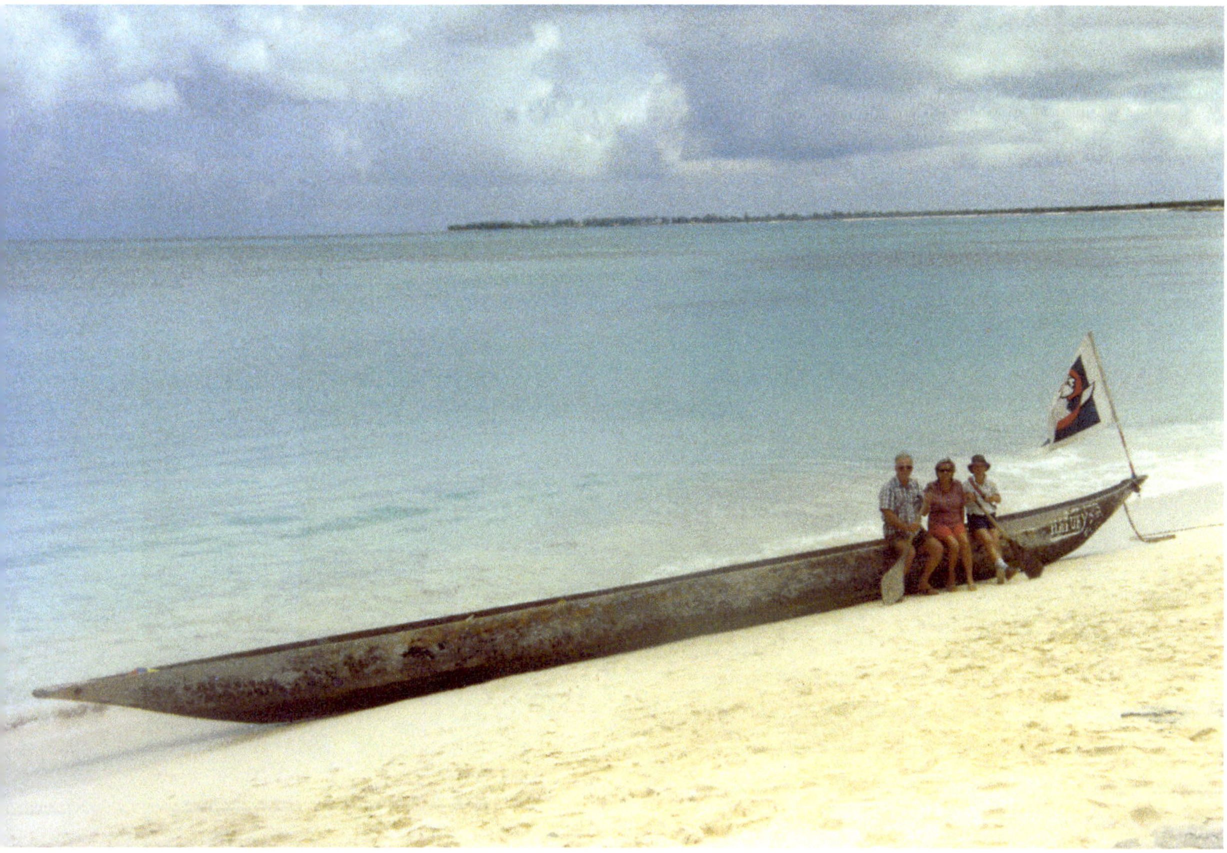

The Play

The play *Paradise Now*, produced in April 2005, served as development for the film. The Play's concept was a "behind the scenes" look at the rehearsal of a ceremony to honor the Spirit of the Taíno. The stage and film crew were part of the cast. The idea was not only to have the audience watch a rehearsal of a play, but also to participate in the ceremony by drumming, chanting and dancing. Images of artifacts and Alton Lowe's paintings projected on a screen enhanced the experience, which in five year's time morphed into the docudrama *Full Circle: A Taíno Story*.

Nathan Rausch, Sound (Play) and Producer (Film) and Travis Neff, Lighting (Play) and Director (Film)

Jason Stoetzer, Anibal "Debo" Herrera, Tiffany "Hanan" Madera, Amy Biaz, Lela Lombardo, Elizabeth Ayoub, Ricky J. Martinez in foreground coming to join the cast on stage.

The Film

A (Fast-) Forward To The Film
Full Circle: A Taíno Story *by The Filmmaker Travis Neff*

In The Beginning...

    I think I have been working in theatre my whole life. I started out wanting to be the next big-named stage actor, but what really excited me was watching what goes on backstage. After graduating from Florida State University with a bachelors degree in Theatre Arts, I moved back to my hometown of Miami, FL and immediately landed a job in the scene shop at Coconut Grove Playhouse. Every time we were loading in a show, I just loved standing at center stage to watch the fly system carry the dusty main curtain out to the grid, revealing the 1100 empty seats and all of the theatre lighting units—so many lights—looking right back at me; I knew that I really wanted to do lighting. I began designing lights for the smaller theatres and, within a few years, had created a niche for myself designing for almost every nonprofit studio, black-box theatre and small drama company from Miami Beach to the boondocks, from Key West to the Bahamas. It didn't take long before my family stopped asking, "Where's Trav?" because they knew: I was in a theatre somewhere, doing some show. I missed countless events, family gatherings, birthday parties (and even, more recently, my brother's wedding).

    I spent one Christmas with Sandra Riley in Green Turtle Cay, Bahamas. Alton Lowe had been producing annual productions for the Abaco Cultural Society, usually during the holidays when he could really gather a crowd. This year, he recruited Sandra to direct a concert, and she recruited me. I had heard that the shows in year's past were lit by a single follow spot, so I thought this was going to be easy and might even turn into a bona fide Caribbean vacation, a real getaway. Nope. This show was no different, plus Sandra was at the helm and I was the shipmate; there was work to be done. I arrived in GTC with a large duffle bag (heavier than my own body weight) filled with 400-feet of cable and 16 par-can fixtures that I had already ordered had come by way of ferry. By Christmas 1996, I had provided the island's Garden Theatre with a fully operational lighting system, just in time for our holiday production.

Road Trip!

In the summer of 1999, I joined Sandra on another trip, this time out West. I was to accompany her and Peggy C. Hall on their annual cross-country camper excursion to a little house tucked up in the mountains of Kooskia, Idaho. As a young boy, I loved the outdoors; and on this trip, I was going to enjoy myself. Find myself. I looked forward

to escaping into the secluded woods, where I would watch wild animals grazing the hillside, inner-tube in the warm river waters, meditate in a sweat lodge under the evening moon, and play a soft drum beat under bright stars. But we had a long way to go to get there, with stops along the way carefully scheduled to allow for the girls' planned jewelry shows, clay and bead art exhibits, and let's not forget the teddy-bear shops and photo ops. So, to document my first road trip across the good ol' U.S. of A, I brought along my brand new journal. I wrote and I wrote and I wrote. And when I tired of that, I actually attempted poetry; I thought I could maybe write a poem as well as Ms. Peg. Needless to say, I probably tortured my lady friends with my stanzéd prose. I mean, they were my former English teachers. But they applauded. They applauded my efforts, anyway. But barely up into the Carolinas, I was already over my journaling and trial poetry. I desperately felt the need to do something, to find a project I could call my own. I picked up one of Sandra's books, *The Lucayans,* and escaped into her poetic prose. I found myself in—for lack of a better word—paradise.

The Readings

Sandra seemed to take notice of my new, keen interest in her novella. I had already picked out my favorite sections, but being the writer and director she was, Sandra had to point out the "important" parts. The two of us sat together and had little orange post-

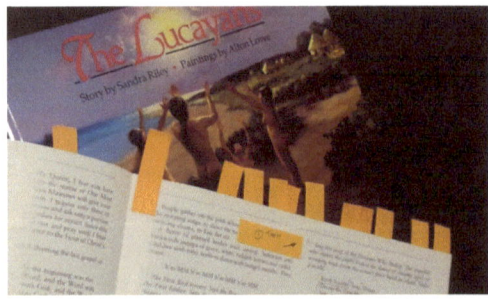

its sticking out from the edges of our books that marked a selection that we were both excited about sharing with interested listeners. As we took turns reading our receptive parts aloud, I was eager to flip the book around to show our spectators the book's paintings by Alton Lowe that so beautifully demonstrated the paradise I frequented.

Post-reading discussions turned into long conversations about the early Caribbean natives, their lifeways, how they tended the Earth, blessed all facets of Nature, communicated with the fish and the birds, the sun and the moon. I wanted to go back in time, and live right there with them, to learn their language, to see life as they saw it, sit by their fires, and learn from their elders. Part of me wanted to ask them questions about "the time before this time." Part of me wanted to make their world come alive again, maybe just for myself at first, but really for everyone. Maybe, as I was so oft to do, I could recreate their world on the stage.

Paradise Now

I came home excited about the idea of a play based on our book readings. As a lighting designer working on the staff at Miami's leading black-box studio, I knew exactly how we could do it. Sandra would write the script and direct, but I needed someone with me behind the Curtain of Oz to create our paradise; I needed an expert in the field of audio and video. Enter Nathan Rausch!

Nate and I shared a hidden passion for film, so we thought it would just be cool to video tape our rehearsal and production process and present that as part of the show, a sort of documentary—not only archiving our project, but adding a new dimension to our presentation. Nate and Sandra and I were having a production meeting to discuss the requirements for our technical elements: sound effects, lighting, and props—which needed to include a single palm tree and kiddie pool to represent "the island" (the Lucayos) as our set. All of a sudden, Nate asked, "Why don't we just make a film?" Sandra and I looked at each other and smiles came to our faces.

In the Spring of 2005, our play production went on as scheduled. We founded The Crystal Parrot Players as a nonprofit organization and received a county grant to stage *Paradise Now*, now! But Nate's question reverberated within us: "Why aren't we making a film?" *Paradise Now: The Movie*—now that sounds like a very exciting project!

Crash Course

Now, I may have 10+ years of professional theatre under my belt, but cinematography is a whole different animal. I needed to learn how to make a film—fast! I enrolled in a Fall course at the local community college. Obviously much older than the freshmen in the class, and being about the same age as my teacher, Mr. Bogdan Heretoiu, it was easy to create a bond with my professor. I could tell he was eager to work on his own craft. He needed a project that would give him the freedom to have his artistry shine through. One afternoon we were hanging out after class and I said to him, "I have a script based on a very special book, and I want you to shoot it for me." OK, so I had to sign a contract with him to come on board as my DP—but hey, someone had to create the shot list. After all, I was essentially asking a professional to put all of the ideas in my little head onto tape!

Africa Hot!

That's what we called it. At least, that's what it felt like to us. It was the summer of 2006 and we were finally shooting! The timing couldn't have been more perfect, thank you Great Spirit, because even the park improvements came to a standstill in such record temperatures. We had an empty beach from sunrise to sunset—just the way I liked it—with no people, no stacks of beach chairs, no whistling lifeguards, no sailboats offshore, not even an occasional passerby. It was us and the natural wildlife, the perfect setting, what a blessing. If we ever had to hold off rolling, it was for the occasional

freighter in the distance or airplane flying overhead, or because makeup was melting. Recorded temperatures at Virginia Key Beach during our shoot were around 86 degrees—but it certainly felt more like 106. It was as if we were on safari, setting up tents with tarps tied up to empty bbq pits; it seemed whenever cameras weren't rolling, we were running for shade.

One Degree of Separation

This was my debut film and I was going to need some help. Bogdan called Massimo Messina (Cam Assist) and my first call was to my girl Jessica Bennett (Production Consultant) to do a site visit with me, because I needed her to…well, to tell me what I needed. She immediately called the hardest worker in the biz, Jorge Kreimer (my Gaffer).

He called Mike Germaine, who donated a truck full of gear for the entire week! And Mike called in my grips and sound guys: Ricardo Barredo, Chris Hill, Juan Linares, Brian Bertrand, and Raul Vidaurre.

Hands down, there is no doubt that I could even function without the undying support of my best friend, Rafael Cubela (Production Coordinator) who was by my side day and night. He handled everything, from catering to pushing the cargo van out of the sand, from relieving the boom op to raking seaweed out of frame. He wooed my mother, Ms. Mary LaMont (Hi Mom!) into lending us her garage tarps, office fans, patio lawn chairs, rakes and brooms and even her backup generator with gasoline—all of which he packed up in the rental truck. And it was Rafa who originally found our makeup crew Puchy and Peachie! Puchy worked at a tanning salon on South Beach and helped turn our Columbian actor Rio Chavarro and Cuban actress Cristina Garcia into the Taínos you see in Alton's book paintings. Puchy made the wigs and dressed our cast of two with thongs and twigs. When we needed a sponge or spritz, we never shouted out "Makeup!" we shouted (with love and laughter) "pUchY!"

A Second Movie, A Whole Different Kind of Beast

I wasn't only going to "make a movie" here. Yes, as a filmmaker, I wanted to bring Sandra's story and Alton's paintings from the book *The Lucayans* alive onto the big screen. But it was equally important to me as a documentarian to balance the spine of the book's story segments of 12 scenes with "talking heads." Over the course of two years, we conducted interviews with individuals who could articulate the history of the Lucayan Taíno people and their culture. So capturing the "docu" portions for the film was just as much of a daunting task as shooting our intimate "drama" scenes on our local beach. We started with interviewing Sandra (whew!) and (finally) Alton in Miami, who explained a lot about the book, and provided the "backdrop." Then I got a chance to ask specific questions and discuss various topics regarding the indigenous people with local archaeologist Bob Carr in Davie, and Dr. Don Gerace in Punta Gorda.

Even then, I wanted an international and scientific take on the subject, with footage of actual petroglyphs at real Taíno sites. So, Sandra and I investigated further, deeper. Her contacts took us back to the Bahamas, where we met with Jock Morgan at the Preacher's Cave Lucayan site in North Eleuthera (with the distinct honor and help of Jane Day, Raymond Harrison, Jackie Gibson, and Alyssa Harrison); and my contacts took us into the mountains of Puerto Rico where we met three more archaeologists at the Taíno museum and preservation sites, Carmen Martinez Aja at Tibes, then Luis Rodriguez and Cesar Velentin at Caguana (all with the guidance of JC Baez, his mom who fed us, and Dr. Luis Diaz at the University in Ponce).

Now I had some balance. Something for Eddie "The Editor" Miyar and me to chew on for two years. But, just when I thought I would call it a "wrap"—even after already having a screening—I wanted MORE! For my "Scene 8" I wanted to execute a green screen and black-box studio pick-up shoot with Ana Mendez and Olvida Alva as Taíno spiritual ancestors with Jessica at the helm this time as DP. In addition, Adam Cronan (our Co-Producer) and I felt that, in this last round, we really needed to take the bar up a notch by including lower-third graphics designed by Javier Chacin. We also needed to make the translation subtitles consistent, which couldn't be done without Jason "MJ" Stoetzer, my BFF, God love him for pouring his heart and soul into so many of my projects.

Tainotí

So during that first summer, I had on location with me: Sandra, Nate, a cast of two, a production crew of twelve, seven PA's and a post-production crew of five, and we recorded five voice-overs. The second unit, two years later, was another cast of two, plus Jess and Eddie, with five new PA's, who helped me make (our) movie magic in 24 hours—that's 44 people for the dramatic portion of the film. Of course, the film would not be possible without CPP's nine additional board members and the generosity of the Negley Flinn Charitable Foundation, Marialaura Leslie and the many folks at Miami-Dade County Department of Cultural Affairs, the inspirational help of the *Paradise Now* cast of six, the 52 Patrons, folks who made cash donations at the door to see our film's premiere, our 45 Donors and Contributors who gave in the hundreds, and 11 Benefactors who contributed in the thousands. Together, we produced successful screening events at four different venues throughout Miami, which would not have been possible without the tremendous help of their hard-working staffs, including the 20 Sponsors and the support of their representatives.

The most special thing about our entire crew was that we were all friends. Maybe I didn't know everybody, but no one did; it was like a family gathering; everyone there was one-degree away from each other. I didn't need to go out of my way to build team camaraderie; Great Spirit already took care of that. Sandra's story and my film is about that which connects each and every one of us to one another, and that is why people wanted to be a part of it. If I add the total number of folks who participated, it's almost 200-degrees! Now that's one HOT film!!! Each and every one of those people is a warrior in my book. And I couldn't have done a thing without Sandra's inspiration. So, in honor of her lifetime of work on the Lucayan Taíno people, I give the entire 10-year project, this film, back to her—FULL CIRCLE! Together, what a journey we have had.

And blessed we were! Blessed by the presence of Catherine "Hummingbird" Ramirez who offered a touching service at our Preview and World Premiere screenings. Movie-goers came from across county lines, even from other states and countries, driving around in crazy traffic to squeeze this one special hour into their busy, worldly lives, and were all graced by Hummingbird's touch, calmed by her burning incense, and silenced by her soothing voice. Audiences had an opportunity to breathe in a moment of meditation and reflection before the film started as she reminded us HOW Great Spirit got us here, together; she reminded us of WHO we are, the Rainbow Warriors that carry a message of peace and unity; and she reminded us WHY we were gathered at that moment—to honor and celebrate these gone, but not forgotten caretakers of our Earth.

fin

Move Forward
by Stepping Backward
Tracing Steps

In 1992, The Bahamas Quincentennial Committee hoped that the five-hundred year anniversary of Columbus meeting the Lucayan Taíno in the Bahamas would bring European, African, Caribbean countries and the Americas together in an atmosphere of peace and love for humankind.

Like indigenous people everywhere, the Hopi of Arizona held that the key to happiness in life, and balance and harmony of the earth and universe was respect for all living things for we are all one, created by one.

With two world wars and the prophesy of a third, the Hopi realized that the survival of the World was at stake. So, in 1948, four Hopi elders made a commitment to deliver this message of peace to the Nations of the World. In October 1991, only one elder remained to fulfill the mission to open the doors of the Great House of Mica (UN) to the native peoples. He delivered a letter and a sacred prayer feather to the office of the General Secretary. On December 10, 1992, he was allowed ten minutes to deliver the Hopi Message to the General Assembly. In 2010 Barack Obama endorsed the United Nations Declaration on the Rights of Indigenous Peoples by saying the "aspirations it affirms—including the respect for the institutions and rich cultures—are ones we must always seek to fulfill." Now The International Day of the World's Indigenous Peoples (August 9) is annually celebrated with forums and interactive dialogues at the UN.

The Sculpture

The Memorial Sculpture Garden at Green Turtle Cay, Abaco, Bahamas and the one at Key West, Florida are notable among master sculptor James Mastin's numerous contributions to the cultural life of the Bahamian people. He has created another sculpture for a proposed monument, this time memorializing the Taíno people who migrated to the Lucayan Islands from islands in the Caribbean prior to Columbus' arrival.

James Mastin's sculpture shows a Taíno family dancing in the water with the dolphins celebrating life. The artist has left a space for us to take hands with them.

The Sculptor
James Mastin

James Mastin is a classically trained artist and sculptor. He refuses to be bound by labels or genres, and his work ranges from tight realism to lyrical abstraction. He uses art as a means of personal exploration. In 1978, he sculpted a portrait bust of Albert Lowe of Green Turtle Cay, The Bahamas, which so impressed Alton Lowe, that he conceived of a dream of a public sculpture garden as a tribute to American Loyalists exiled to the Bahamas after the Revolutionary War.

James sculpted the busts in the Memorial Sculpture Garden in Green Turtle Cay, which was declared a National Monument of The Bahamas in 1987. People attended the opening celebration from the United States, Canada and the Bahamas. The Police Band played, the local community dressed in period costumes and danced in the streets. The Memorial Sculpture Garden consists of a central monument, *The Landing*, which depicts two life-sized young women, loyal to the British Crown, at the moment of their arrival in the Bahamas after fleeing from the American colonies in 1783. The central monument is surrounded by some three dozen bronze portrait busts of twentieth century descendants of families who were among the early settlers to the Bahama Islands. The Memorial Sculpture Garden is a tribute to the courage of those who left everything behind to begin new lives in an untamed wilderness. Constructed of cast bronze, native stone and grasses, *The Landing* anchors the Sculpture Garden, which extends across 5000 square feet arranged in the pattern of the British flag in the historic business district in New Plymouth, Green Turtle Cay, Abaco. Each portrait bust in the Garden took weeks to create. Working from old photographs, advice from family members, and live modeling sessions whenever possible, James crafted uncanny likenesses and emotional auras of each honoree in painstaking detail, using a proprietary mixture of clay and wax that he has developed for this purpose. Using the "lost wax" process, James had the foundry cast each piece from molten bronze. After the bronze cools, James applied a chemical patina onto the bronze portrait to protect it and to alter the natural golden color.

Years before the creation of the Loyalist Memorial Sculpture Garden, James began a long and varied relationship with the cultural life of The Bahamas, which began in 1975, when he collaborated with Bahamian painter Alton Roland Lowe in the founding of the Albert Lowe Museum in Green Turtle Cay, Abaco. Hundreds of Bahamians and foreigners participated in the celebrations when the Museum opened to the public. Dignitaries from Canada and the Bahamian government attended. James collaborated with Alton Lowe on many cultural events in the Abacos, helping to arrange for lectures, and showcasing entertainers including an American chorale, a dance company, a theatrical troupe as well as local Bahamian performers. For decades, he also participated in an annual art exhibit in Nassau. He volunteered to help organize the first Sister City Festival in Green Turtle Cay which celebrated the island's shared cultural heritage with Key West, Florida and which has become an annual event, alternating between The Bahamas and Key West, attracting hundreds of tourists. For more than two decades, James organized and sang in Christmas concerts held in Green Turtle Cay, occasionally bringing the concert to other islands in the Abacos. In 2005 he created a series of paintings for The Bahamas Postal Service stamp edition celebrating the Olympic Games.

James has also created historical public sculpture parks in the United States. Located in Key West, Florida, sister city to New Plymouth, Green Turtle Cay, the Key West Historical Sculpture Garden, which opened in 1997, honors the bravery of the men who made their living in the wrecking industry that made Key West the wealthiest city in the United States south of New York in the nineteenth century. The central monument, *The Wreckers,* depicts two men rescuing cargo and a young passenger from a sinking ship. It is surrounded by over three dozen bronze portrait busts of individuals who contributed to the development of Key West, including Henry Flagler, Ernest Hemingway, Stephen Mallory, and President Harry Truman. In Savannah, Georgia, James created a life-sized tableau in Benjamin Franklin Square, which commemorates the Haitian Volunteers who fought in the American Revolutionary war. The monument depicts six Haitian soldiers in the heat of battle, fighting under the flag of France alongside American colonists during the Battle of Savannah. Each soldier displays the pathos of the moment; one is wounded and one watches in horror while the others bravely maintain their battle stations. Installed in 2010, the monument has become a must-see tourist destination in Savannah.

James' personal work ranges from the allegorical to the prophetic. He exhibits in numerous South Florida venues, and welcomes visitors to his studio in Miami, Florida and to his website www.jamesmastinart.com. Besides the Memorial Sculpture Garden, Mastin's work can also be seen at the Albert Lowe Museum (242-365-4094) and the Lowe Art Gallery, Green Turtle Cay, Abaco (242-365-4264).

We all were saddened by the passing of James Mastin on July 24, 2016, but take comfort in knowing that his art lives on.

The Painter
Alton Roland Lowe

If I had been asked when I left The Bahamas at sixteen to become an artist what I hoped to achieve in life, I would have been hard pressed to provide an answer. Like my own country whose sense of identity developed slowly over many decades, culminating in self-government in 1967 and independence in 1973, my own vision of who I was and what I could accomplish in life came slowly. Those first sixteen years, however, were truly formative years, and they have molded and enriched my life to this day.

In those early years, I took for granted, as did most Bahamians, the unique beauty which surrounded me as I grew up. It was only after leaving The Bahamas to study in the United States that I slowly realized what a marvelous place my country was and to this day remains, and this has profoundly affected my work. An artist can paint anything anywhere. His talent is only limited by his vision. As many people know, I have chosen to paint primarily Bahamian subjects year after year. I have done this out of a great love for The Bahamas, its people and its heritage. It is my intent and my vision to amass a body of work that over time will show people for generations to come what The Bahamas was, is, and can become.

My interest in our traditions took shape when I was twelve years old and organized the Empire Day celebrations on Green Turtle Cay. It amazes me, and even makes me laugh to think of the "old" people allowing me to do so. I designed the costumes, organized the plaiting of the maypole, got older people to recite original poems and to sing island ballads. At this time and later, I was also active in Green Turtle Cay's New Year's Day "Bunce Parades", once again designing costumes and organizing the parade.

In 1976, one of the proudest moments of my life occurred when I established the Albert Lowe Museum at Green Turtle Cay. I was determined that the wonderful stories I had heard as a boy would not be lost. The museum, named in honour of my ship-building father, was meant to be a place that could tell the story of these islands and its early people: the Lucayans, the Loyalists and their descendants, and the slaves who accompanied them and became the backbone of the country. This was the first museum in The Bahamas. At times it has been a struggle financially to keep the museum open, but over the years, tourists and journalists from all over the world have come to the museum and learned about our history and culture. Those who are interested know that The Bahamas is much more than "sand, sea and sun". Today, not only tourists, but numerous groups of students from the Out Islands and Nassau visit the museum to learn about their past. It has become a very useful educational tool and continues to energize me in terms of our history and our environment. Although I have never received government financial support, I would like to say that The Bahamas Government has always fully supported this effort. Indeed, the museum was officially opened by Sir Clement Maynard and opening ceremonies were attended by hundreds of people from throughout the island and abroad.

Many good things flowed from establishing the museum. Bahamians from Green Turtle Cay and neighbouring islands took renewed interest in family genealogy. I established committees and worked with officials in Nassau, principally in the Ministry of Tourism under Sir Clement Maynard and officials in Key West, Florida (where many Bahamians have relatives), to develop a program to reunite families which had long since lost contact with each other. This was the original Island Roots Festival. Hundreds of people participated on both sides of the Gulf Stream. Ceremonies took place both on Green Turtle Cay and in Key West. The Bahamas Government fully supported these efforts. This always included high-ranking official representation and support. As part of the first year's program, officials on both sides established Green Turtle Cay and Key West as "Sister Cities". Throughout the years, these festivities have been covered by ZNS as well as Miami's Channels 10 and 4.

A second major result of establishing the museum was a renewed interest in archaeology, making sense of artifacts readily available from Lucayan days and early settlements of Loyalists. A close friend, Robert Carr, an internationally respected archaeologist, organized a dig which located the early settlement of Carleton on Great Abaco. His work continues up to the present. In April 2003, he sent a group to analyze the area at the New Plymouth jail in Green Turtle Cay. Additionally, he has excavated material on the museum grounds and helped authenticate and date materials now at the museum. Recently the government hired Bob Carr to excavate Preacher's Cave at Eleuthera where they discovered Lucayan artifacts and material from the Eleutheran Adventurers.

A third result was the publication in 1983 of Sandra Riley's book *Homeward Bound: A History of the Bahama Islands to 1850* and contains a definitive study of Abaco in the American Loyalist Plantation Period. The book remains in print and has helped preserve information which might well have been lost. Her research material is archived at the museum.

Finally, the fourth significant result of opening the museum and the growing interest in the past was the creation of the Memorial Sculpture Garden at Green Turtle Cay.

I had dreamed for years of creating a sculpture garden which would celebrate the landing of the Loyalists and their slaves in The Bahamas. The Garden's basic design is in the form of the Union Jack. Placed at intervals are pedestals with bronze busts of descendents of the early settlers. A bronze plaque on each pedestal tells an individual's story. Centered in the Garden are two young ladies in bronze standing atop a large pedestal. The bronzes are all created by my friend, James Mastin. The center sculpture was entitled by Mastin *The Landing*. Groundbreaking ceremonies under the auspices of Lady Pindling gave a strong start to a project which took fully four years to complete. The Garden is a monument to Loyalists and slaves alike. Both started new lives and became something unique: neither British nor African, but something new—Bahamian. The Garden, which was officially opened by Sir Clement Maynard in 1987, was declared a Bahamas National Monument and today attracts hundreds of tourists. It has been written up in dozens of articles published in newspapers and magazines around the world. As a proud Bahamian, I might add that the Garden was the model for another Sculpture Garden created at Key West several years ago. I would also like to say that without the financial support of many people in Nassau and other islands, neither the idea nor the work of sculptor James Mastin would have ever seen the light of day.

Two other areas of interest should be mentioned as being solid contributions to Bahamian society and culture. I have always been interested in the performing arts and for twenty-eight years have sponsored a cultural weekend at Christmas. Concerts, plays and talks have been organized over the years. Community support has been little short of magnificent, and audiences come from islands near and far. The annual weekend is supported by the Ministry of Tourism and information is widely disseminated through various publications. Many foreigners schedule their visits to coincide with the weekend. Performers are both foreign and Bahamian. Recently, Key West sent a seventy-member Chorale for the occasion and Miami's Momentum Ballet Company has twice brought its troupe to perform under American grants to their company.

While these activities have enriched my own life and that of many others, my main work and interest continues to be painting in oils. As of today, I have held thirty-eight one-man shows in Nassau. I have also recently opened up a gallery at my home on Black Sound, Green Turtle Cay, which is open for special exhibitions of my work throughout the year and by appointment when otherwise closed. I would like to think that the paintings which I have created through the years make up a body of work that uniquely tells the story of this beautiful land and her remarkable people. Life has been rich in these islands, but it has also been hard. Weak men and women would not have survived. Indeed, many of the strong did not survive. I have spent years recording in oils the lives of white and black Bahamians. While many of these paintings are now in private hands, I expect that over time many will come into public view, and the world will see what a rich legacy has been left to future generations.

I would be remiss if I did not discuss the stamp paintings, now numbering over one hundred. These have taken even me by surprise. The first set of four "Loyalist" paintings was done in 1983. Working with the Postmaster General at the time, John Saunders, I have produced paintings expressly for The Bahamas Government almost every year since. It has been a labour of love. I take great pride and am grateful to the Government for having had the opportunity to be of service to my country in this way.

Summing up, people still marvel at the rich colours in my paintings, but these are true to life, as true as anything ever painted anywhere. I have sought to capture men and women at work and play, in all walks of life. I have done extensive research for my historical paintings, whether shipbuilding in the Abacos or Columbus landing at San Salvador. Old buildings, many sadly now gone, are forever memorialized. The beauty of our country shown in seascapes and landscapes, at dawn and at sunset, even in the luminous light of the moon, have, I believe, awakened many of us to the need to preserve what we have for future generations. These paintings have also served as "ambassadors of good will" for many people who either see them in private homes, public institutions or through the hundreds of articles in newspapers and magazines as well as television interviews done over the years. I have loved this country and discover each year new reasons for continuing my work. Many of my paintings, especially the tropical flowers and plants, are purchased for their beauty. These paintings also hold a truth: we must preserve and enhance what God gave us in these islands. I have developed a vision as I have matured and my paintings are at the core of that vision.

The Writer
Sandra Riley

Warm weather has determined the course of my life. After living through seventeen freezing Great Lake winters in Grosse Pointe, I chose to attend Barry College in Miami, Florida over Sienna Heights in Adrian, Michigan. I arrived with no major study in mind. My advisor, a professor of theatre, suggested I take her introduction to drama course and pursue a degree in theatre studies. As a graduation gift in 1960, my mother took me to Nassau in the Bahamas. Wandering away from the British Colonial I came to a deserted field. Gazing out to sea, I knelt and felt an emotion so deep it brought me to tears. I didn't know why or how, but I felt that whatever I was to do with my life had to do with this place, this Bahamas.

Having the advantage of looking back over a half century, I know now why certain twists and turns occurred along the journey of my life and what I learned from those experiences in order to have done the work I did and continue to do. Between 1960 and 1973 I sustained life and fed my passion as a high school drama teacher by day and community theatre director by night. In school by seven and out of the theatre by eleven. Hialeah High/Barn Theatre in Miami Lakes, then Miami Springs High/Players Theatre in Coconut Grove. During the first three summers I took a Master of Arts degree in theatre at the University of Michigan. Throughout those years I directed forty plays. In the early 60s, Hialeah High had a band and an orchestra director, two choral directors, two dance teachers and myself, so we did *Finian's Rainbow*, *The King and I*, *Oklahoma* and *South Pacific*. The last two were also performed at Dade County Auditorium (Miami's Arsht center of the day). Highlights of the Barn Theatre include *The Rainmaker*, *The Miracle Worker* and *A Streetcar Named Desire*. At Miami Springs High it was *The Crucible* and *The Romantics*. For The Players Theatre, I directed *The Andersonville Trial*, *The Fantasticks* and Anouilh's *Antigone* featuring a young Sylvester Stallone as Haemon. I needed a change so I took a one-year position teaching drama and directing plays overseas at Camp Zama, Japan. I climbed Mt. Fuji in the fall and toured Sapporo during their Ice Festival. Japan was cold. I know now that this year abroad was a transition in my spiritual as well as my work life. I was captivated by the mysterious Far East, yet I felt a strong pull to go home.

To what? My drama position was no longer available, only basic English classes. A college friend put me in touch with the Board Chair of The Fort Lauderdale Children's Theatre whose husband's investment corporation owned a land development company on the island of San Salvador in the Bahamas. At my interview, I was told that the company was looking for someone to do historical research into Columbus, pirates, and the exiled American Loyalists whose ruined plantation buildings dotted the island. When asked for my qualifications to do this kind of work I said, "I am a dramaturge. I analyze dramatic literature. It's my job to investigate the historical and cultural facets of the society and the environment of the place as well as the physical and psychological aspects of the people involved." Columbus Landings hired me and flew me to San Salvador on the company plane. I drove the King's Highway avoiding pot holes and gasping at views of the sea. The island was ten degrees hotter than Miami and a major fork in the road for me. Back at home, I searched the libraries, read everything on all topics, trying to get a handle on the scope of the work. I soon realized that any branch of any one of these topics had been for some scholars a lifetime of work. It was the recession of 1973 and my time was running out with Columbus Landings who kept me on for little pay, but with travel expenses. Daunted by the wealth of research material, I left the study of Columbus to other scholars. Instead, at the Smithsonian Anthropological Library, I asked for information on the pre-Columbian people of the Caribbean and the Bahamas. Guided through rooms and rooms containing bins and bins of bones, I was seated at a small desk near one filing cabinet and given a folder. One of the monographs I read was "The Arawack Language of Guiana" written in 1871 by D. G. Brinton M. D. I wasn't the only one working out of field. My life-long research would focus on the people who greeted Columbus. As expected, I was fired. After all, who needs a historian in a period of economic stagnation? I maintained an off-and-on relationship with the company through the 70s, actually finished the map I was working on and wrote a self-guided tour of San Salvador for them.

Over the next ten years I continued research on my own time. Teaching English at Coral Gables High with no theatre work and summers off allowed me to track down the stories of the American Loyalists in London, the Carolinas, Georgia, Florida, Nassau and New York archives. Locked behind metal gates in the Rare Book Room of the New York Public Library, I found the primary source of the many books on piracy I had read, Captain Charles Johnson's *A General History of the Pyrates* (1724). The lives of the women pirates Anne Bonny and Mary Read fascinated me. The novel I wrote about them was first published in 1980, the year I met Alton Lowe, who encouraged me to write a history of the Bahamas with a focus on the American Loyalists of Abaco. I took a leave of absence from teaching. Alton called every morning asking, "What are you up to? How's it going?" He read every chapter. I took out a loan and self-published *Homeward Bound* in 1983, the year of the Bicentennial of the arrival of the American Loyalists in the Bahamas. During a month's research stay in Nassau, I had met a man on the planning board which selected artists to paint scenes for postage stamps. The Postmaster General contacted Alton to do a series of Loyalist paintings for the Bicentennial. Alton and James Mastin were, at the time, working on a Memorial Sculpture Garden at Green Turtle Cay. Alton asked me to write all the bronze plaques for the Garden and put together a book for the opening ceremony in 1987.

In 1988, the Postmaster General asked Alton to do a series of paintings of the people who greeted Columbus in the Bahamas for the Quincentennial and sent us to San Salvador to do research for the paintings. Macmillan Caribbean commissioned a book telling the story of the Lucayan Taíno people to accompany Alton's stamp paintings. This required me to review and update my research before writing. The International Baccalaureate program came to Gables High and was coupled with the Advanced Placement English, which I team taught with Peggy C. Hall. We spent summers in Idaho working on our literature syllabus, including Native American history, myths and poetry. Out West I attended sweat lodges and drum circles. At a medicine wheel ceremony in Oregon I touched my forehead to the earth and experienced a flood of emotion like the one at Nassau in 1960. I realized that my connecting with nature this way was essential preparation for the writing. I needed to be in the classroom by 7 a.m. so I rose at 2 a.m. and for those few quiet hours I wrote *The Lucayans*. It was published in 1991. I was invited to organize and report on the General Literature papers at the 47th International Congress of Americanists held that year at Tulane University in New Orleans where I also presented a dramatic reading of my prose-poem novella.

The next year an IB Theatre Arts class was added to my schedule. This program was a rigorous course of study for students which included written research papers and oral exams. Until I retired in 1997 I directed *Skin of our Teeth, The Madwoman of Chaillot, The Comedy of Errors* and *On the Verge*. Alton had seen a few of these productions and wanted to include plays as part of his cultural activities on Green Turtle Cay. I directed two one-act plays for him. Alton, never short of an idea which would put me to work, next suggested that I write a play about a Green Turtle Cay woman who goes to school in Key West in the late 1880s. *Miss Ruby* was produced at his gallery in 2000. I never imagined when I started my research on the Bahamas that I would write plays based on it, but that is exactly what happened. The early English settlers of the mid-1600s through the Great Age of Piracy surfaced as *Matt Lowe*. The Crystal Parrot Players, a nonprofit company, performed both plays in Miami and Key West. A third solo play, *Mariah Brown*, based on the early Bahamian pioneer to Coconut Grove, premiered in Miami in 2003. I published the historical solo plays as *Bahamas Trilogy* in 2010 and *Mariah Brown* premiered in the Bahamas at the 2011 Shakespeare in Paradise Festival in Nassau.

In 2016, Miami's New Theatre produced the World Premiere of *Footprints*, my play about the Coconut Grove pioneers, Mary Barr and Kirk Munroe. One performance at the Woman's Club of Coconut Grove honored the 125th anniversary of the Club's founding. As a dramatist it is thrilling for me to see history come to life in theatrical performances. The hotter, the better.

Circles
by Peggy C. Hall

I am dreaming of circles, rings
of neon hoops around our Moon,
whose pock-marked, cicatrized face
illuminates each medicine wheel,
shaken from its old, old bed.
Thousands of years each site has lain
sleeping sacred under Mother Earth.

Now I'm seeing ancient tribal scars
scooped and shaped around each rim:
Aureoles on this Great Mother,
opened to life by praying men
helping Solar Father join his bride
through her limestoned-hymened skin,
pressing inward, fulfilling life,
wedding
fire-ringed Earth
to rainbowed Sky.

FULL CIRCLE: A Taíno Story

FULL CIRCLE: A Taíno Story is a study of the cosmology and cultural heritage of the indigenous people of the Caribbean on the brink of European contact. The disease, genocide, and ecocide that followed in the wake of Columbus' arrival eliminated several million Lucayan Taíno from the Bahamas, and Taíno from Hispañola, Jamaica, Cuba and Puerto Rico.

Full Circle: A Taíno Story is an authentic portrayal of their lifeways interwoven with paintings of Lucayan Taíno life as well as interviews from leading scholars:

ALTON LOWE – Internationally known Bahamian artist whose paintings illustrate the book *The Lucayan Taíno: First People of the Bahamas*.

BOB CARR – Florida and Caribbean Archaeologist, President of the Archaeological & Historical Conservancy, Davie, Florida.

SANDRA RILEY – Researcher of the Bahamas and its History, Author of *The Lucayan Taíno: First People of the Bahamas*.

DR. DON GERACE – Founder, Field Study Program (Finger Lakes College, NY) on San Salvador, Bahamas.

LUIS RODRIGUEZ – Head Archaeologist, Tibes and Caguana sites, Puerto Rico Institute of Culture; Sub-Chief, General Council of Taínos.

JOCK MORGAN – President, Historical Society of North Eleuthera and Field Coordinator of Preacher's Cave.

CRYSTAL PARROT and BAMA FILMS
in association with ZENDEN PRODUCTIONS and INDIE OPEN presents
"FULL CIRCLE: A TAÍNO STORY" A documentary film Written and Directed by TRAVIS NEFF
Based on the novel "THE LUCAYANS" and the stage play "PARADISE NOW" by SANDRA RILEY
Starring CHRISTINA GARCIA and RIO CHAVARRO with Special Appearances by OLVIDA ALVA and ANA MENDEZ
Including the Voice Talents of MARIO ERNESTO SANCHEZ as Christopher Columbus, LAVERNE LEWIS-CUZZOCREA as Taíno Preist,
M.J. STOETZER as Latin Preist, TORRENCE WELCH as Hatuey, TIFFANY "HANAN" MADERA as Anacaona
Director of Photography BOGDAN HERETOIU, Editors EDUARDO MIYAR and NATHAN RAUSCH
Original Score by NATHAN RAUSCH, Language by JASON STOETZER, Original Song by ELIZABETH AYOUB & RON TAYLOR
Executive Producer SANDRA RILEY Producers TRAVIS NEFF, ADAM CRONAN and NATHAN RAUSCH
Sponsored by THE NEGLEY FLINN CHARITABLE FOUNDATION

crystalparrot.org

NOT SUGGESTED VIEWING FOR YOUNG CHILDREN

www.ingramcontent.com/pod-product-compliance
Lightning Source LLC
Chambersburg PA
CBHW041514220426
43668CB00002B/17